The ABCs of English Grammar:

A Twenty-First Century Handbook

Ron Rothnie, M.A.

rothniehome@shaw.ca
Fax (250) 477-2480

National Library of Canada Cataloguing in Publication Data

Rothnie, Ronald Coutts
  The ABCs of English grammar

  Includes index.
  ISBN 1-895332-33-8

  1. English language–Grammar–Handbooks, manuals, etc. I. Title.
PE1112.R67 2001   428.2   C2001-911327-7

Editorial assistance provided by Susan Lawrence vanisletrails@uniserve.com

Book Design by Desktop Publishing Ltd. Victoria, BC   desktoppublishing@shaw.ca

In Appreciation of

Wanda Alexia Gray Rothnie,
who always went beyond ordinary expectations,

and

Susan Lawrence,
who still does.

After teaching English to students from intermediate through college levels for many years, I wrote *The ABCs of English Grammar: A Twenty-First Century Handbook* for independent students of all ages—for those between twelve and ninety! My aim is to offer some basics in the English language so that learners can refresh, improve, or even gain new skills in spoken and written English.

The ABCs of English Grammar: A Twenty-First Century Handbook is designed to be a self-directed study containing basic information and rules of grammar, practice exercises, an answer key, a glossary (for a few terms that might be unfamiliar), and an index. Although I have planned the content sequentially, there is no reason why a student couldn't refer directly to the Table of Contents, or the Index, to locate information regarding specific concerns or questions.

Several school teachers and university instructors in English have studied the manuscript of *The ABCs of English Grammar: A Twenty-First Century Handbook* and have completed the exercises. All have recommended it highly, so I offer it to students of the language. As an English professor once told our class, "The English grammatical system, if you're lucky, works about 90% of the time."

I have tried to use examples which are within that "90% of the time" with hopes that you will find 100% satisfaction with *The ABCs of English Grammar: A Twenty-First Century Handbook.*

Ron Rothnie

Contents

Chapter I – Parts of Speech – Part I

Chapter 2 – Parts of Speech – Part II

Chapter 3 – Sentence Structure

Chapter 4 – Sentence Tones

Chapter 5 – Punctuation

Chapter 6 – Phrases

Chapter 7 – Functions of Speech

Chapter 8 – Extra Practice Exercises

The ABCs of English Grammar

Chapter 9 – The Ten Most Common Errors in the English Language

Chapter 10 – A Few Additions for Enrichment

Chapter I

Parts of Speech
Part I

Why Use Parts of Speech?

Each word in the English language can be used as one or more parts of speech. Whether a student is in the intermediate grades or at a university level, this system is the most common method used for a basic understanding of the structure of the language. What part of speech a word is depends on how it is used in a sentence. The system isn't foolproof, but it can offer great benefits to a person's proper use of the English language, both spoken and written.

Referring to the Dictionary

The entry words in a dictionary are followed, usually, by the phonetic pronunciation of the word in parentheses (curved lines); next, a part of speech is listed for the word, such as n. (nouns), v.i. or v.t. (verbs), adj. (adjectives), and adv. (adverbs). Sometimes, a word can be used as more than one part of speech, depending on how it is used in a sentence. The next few segments should begin to reduce any confusion on this subject. Finally, some dictionaries give information about the origins and development of meanings for some words; this is called the etymology of words.

Nouns

Definition

A noun is a part of speech which indicates the name of a person (such as *woman* or *father*), place (*Toronto, home*), thing (*car, muffin*), or idea (*peace, conflict*).

Proper Nouns

A proper noun is a noun which indicates the name of a particular person (*Harry*), place (*Vancouver*), or thing (*Eiffel Tower*). Proper nouns are always capitalized.

Common Nouns

A common noun is the name of a class, or category of person, place, thing, or idea (*woman, city, omelet, joy*). If "the" or "a" or "an" precedes a word and can pair up with it successfully, that word is a common noun.

Examples:
a. (the) woman

b. (a) city

c. (an) omelet

d. (the) beauty

Common nouns are not capitalized unless they begin a sentence or a quotation. (See page 61, Example a.)

Exercise 1—Nouns

Write each of the sentences and underline the common and proper nouns, or just list the number of each sentence and write the nouns each contains.

1. The group swam in Lake Okanagan on Friday.

2. The boy bought a Speedo and goggles at the store.

3. When I drove the tractor into the barn, I knew my father would be angry.

4. Mr. Jackson usually spent every day of the summer wrestling alligators.

5. My family saw Grant Hill play basketball.

6. Uncle Duncan came at Christmas and brought my brother a lot of presents.

7. When the Nakanishis visited British Columbia, they went to Long Beach and Victoria.

8. My friends picked strawberries last summer and said their backs ached from the work.

9. With a sailboat, Jill has no need of a motor.

10. When Bobby goes to the fair, he has a ball.

   (Answers to Exercise 1 on page 106)

Exercise 2—Nouns

Follow the instructions for Exercise 1.

1. "Ed, would you like another dish of yogurt?"

2. In the barn, the cat had a feast of rats.

3. The girl loved making models of biplanes and triplanes.

4. Andrea loves swimming and fishing.

5. Her parents tried to prepare the girl for the worst news of her life.

6. There were hundreds of people held by guerrillas at the Japanese Embassy in Lima, Peru.

7. Martin and Jack went to Whistler, British Columbia, for a vacation.

8. "This sentence has a total of five nouns, according to my count," the student said.

9. The group was told that their first dance would take place the following week.

10. At the restaurant, the students proved that their eyes weren't bigger than their stomachs.

   (Answers on page 106)

Pronouns

Definition

A pronoun is a word used in place of a noun or as a word that refers to something or someone without naming it.

Examples:

a. Annie was nice; *she* always gave us a smile.

(In this sentence, "she" is a pronoun, and replaces the noun, "Annie," which is the antecedent, or the noun to which the pronoun refers. "Us" is also a pronoun which stands for one or more nouns which are not named.)

b. *Who* is singing?

(In this sentence, "who" refers to a person without naming him or her.)

Personal Pronouns

The pronouns *I, you, he, she, it, we, they* with all their forms (*me, mine, ours, us*, etc.) are called personal pronouns. When the word *self* or *selves* is added to a form of the personal pronoun, the resultant form (*myself, yourself, himself, herself, themselves*) is called a compound personal pronoun. Such pronouns may be **reflexive** (I hurt *myself*) or **intensive** (President Bush *himself* will be speaking at the meeting.)

Example:

He sees *me*.

(Although included in the personal pronouns' group, "it" is often used impersonally, as in the sentence, "It was cold last night.")

The ABCs of English Grammar

Relative Pronouns

Words used as relative pronouns are: *who, whoever, whom, whomever, what, whatever, which, whichever, whose,* and *that.* The relative pronouns may:

1. Take the place of an antecedent (the word to which the pronoun refers) as follows:

   Whoever comes late will be sorry.

   (Here the relative pronoun "whoever" takes the place of a noun.)

2. Introduce a dependent clause:

   Whatever she says, I will accept it.

   (Leave this until page 34 and information on dependent clauses.)

Interrogative Pronouns

The interrogative pronouns are: *who, whom, whose, which,* and *what.* They are used to introduce a direct question or an indirect question.

Examples:

a. Direct Question: They asked me, "*Who* has stolen the money?"

b. Indirect Question: They asked me *who* had stolen the money.

Demonstrative Pronouns

The four demonstrative pronouns are: *this, that, these,* and *those,* and are used to point out, or call attention to, some particular person, place, or thing.

Examples:

a. *This* is the last stop.

b. *Those* are not Elvis' skates; *these* are.

Indefinite Pronouns

Indefinite pronouns are pronouns that don't refer to specific persons, places, or things. These can be particularly confusing. Some indefinite pronouns are: *any, few, everyone, nobody, nothing, either, many, none, something, anything, no one, each, several, much, all*.

Examples:

a. *Each* of the children complained.

b. I heard *somebody*.

IMPORTANT NOTE:
A **substantive** is a word used to include nouns and pronouns.

Exercise 3—Pronouns

On separate paper, list the number of each sentence and write the pronouns each contains.

1. "I don't care what you say!" Gordon yelled. "This is mine!"

2. They came and visited.

3. When we saw them, we talked about this and that.

4. Jessica said that she could come.

5. Those are yours; this is mine.

6. It is extremely hot in Niagara today.

7. She looked at everyone. "Some of you have not been nice and will be punished."

8. As they came towards her, she laughed.

9. "Each of us must do what he can," the old man told them.

10. We may eat whatever we wish, for these are ours.

(Answers on page 107)

Exercise 4—Pronouns

Follow the instructions for Exercise 1 on Pronouns.

1. "This is the last time I will call any of you to the table!" Mr. Taylor declared loudly.

2. They swallowed something poisonous.

3. Some of them tried, but none succeeded.

4. "Is this ours?" he asked.

5. He saw many of them in the woods.

6. "We haven't seen those," they said, "but we have seen these."

7. "Which do you want?" the man asked me.

8. It is not mine, but I wish it were.

9. All of us hope that Yuko will come.

10. Everybody wanted to know who had stolen it.

(Answers on page 107)

Verbs ———————————————

Definition

Verbs are words that express action, occurrence, or a state of being, whether in the past, present, or future. Each verb in the examples is underlined twice.

Examples:

a. She <u>kicks</u> the ball. (present action)

b. She <u>kicked</u> the ball. (past action)

c. She <u>will</u> <u>kick</u> the ball. (future action)

d. She <u>is</u> a good player. (present state of being)

e. All of us <u>were</u> human. (past state of being)

f. There <u>were</u> men who <u>lived</u> there. (The first verb indicates past state of being; the second verb indicates past action.)

The Four Principal Parts of the Verb

Four principal parts of the verb refers to the forms for the tenses of a verb. Verb tense is the means, or way, by which a verb indicates the time when events occur or conditions exist.

Examples:

a. Harry <u>eats</u>. (present tense)

b. Harry <u>ate</u>. (simple past tense)

The present and simple past tense are two of the four principal parts of the verb. (The other two parts are the past participle and the present participle, which are detailed on page 9.)

Regular Verbs

A regular verb is one for which the past tense and past participle are formed by the addition of –d or -ed to the root form, or present tense form of the verb as in *love/loved* or *climb/climbed*. Verbs are listed in the present tense form in a dictionary and, in order to save time, space and money, the publishers of dictionaries do not usually list these regular verb endings.

Examples:

like, jump

These are the root forms of two regular verbs in the present tense. After such entry words in the dictionary, there will be parentheses enclosing information on the phonetic pronunciation, followed by v.i. or v.t., which indicates that the word is a verb ("v.i." and "v.t." are explained on page 77).

Irregular Verbs

Examples:

a. I swim across the river.

b. I throw the ball.

These two verbs are the root forms of irregular verbs in the present tense. Beyond the information given for regular verbs, an irregular verb changes in some way for other tenses. (See *Past and Present Participles* below.) For the above examples, the simple past forms are swam and threw. ("I swam yesterday" or "I threw the ball yesterday.") In most dictionaries, all irregular verb forms are listed.

Past and Present Participles

The past participle is the third principal part of a verb. If the verb is regular, all that is required for the past tense is the addition of -*d* or -*ed* to the present tense form (*liked, jumped*). If the verb is irregular, and the past participle is different from the past tense, it will be listed directly after the past tense in the dictionary. When using a participle form of the verb, one or more auxiliary, or helping verbs, must be used before the participle.

Examples:

a. He had burped. (Here "burped" is the past participle with "had" used as the auxiliary verb.)

b. He should have noticed the broken window. (Here "noticed" is the past participle with "should" and "have" used as auxiliary verbs.)

The final principal part of the verb is the present participle, which consists of adding -ing to the present tense. The removal of a letter may be required before adding the -ing such as "become" to "becoming."

In the dictionary, if the verb is irregular, the form of the present participle is listed directly after the past participle. (Remember, there may be a single form for both the simple past form and the past participle.)

Examples:

a. He is smiling. (Here "smiling" is the present participle with "is" used as the auxiliary verb.)

b. He has been regarding the broken window. (Here "regarding" is the present participle with "has" and "been" used as the auxiliary verbs.)

It's important to remember that auxiliary verbs are always necessary when using a participle.

A More Detailed Look at Verb Tenses

There are six tenses by which a verb can indicate the time when events or conditions exist. The six tenses are as follows:

Tense	Form
Present	I ask (or) I am asking (or) I do ask
Past	I asked (or) I was asking (or) I did ask
Future	I shall ask (or) I shall be asking
Present Perfect	I have asked (or) I have been asking
Past Perfect	I had asked (or) I had been asking
Future Perfect	I shall have asked (or) I shall have been asking

In the examples, the three perfect tenses are made up from the past participle "asked," or the present participle "asking," plus one or more of the auxiliary verbs *have/had, be/been, shall/will.* (See pages 79 and 99 for more information on shall and will.) The only verb that must be used as an auxiliary verb in a perfect verb tense is some form of the verb *have.*

Exercise 5—Verbs

Write each of the sentences and double underline the auxiliary and main verbs, or just list the number of each sentence and write the verbs each contains.

1. Fumiko smiled when she saw the size of it.

2. Franz had cooked the cat when he was starving.

3. She has skated for three hours.

4. She has burned her left buttock.

5. The family had gone to a counsellor.

6. The family should have gone to a psychiatrist.

7. We could have spotted the mouse if we had looked.

8. I shall ask him for money.

9. Everybody at the picnic had eaten.

10. We will see him next week.

(Answers on page 108)

Exercise 6—Verbs

Write the number of each sentence and list the auxiliary and main verbs that each contains.

1. She has lit the bonfire.

2. They have been asking for the money.

3. I shall have danced in public.

4. The boy could have played in the game if he had been in town.

5. She may have guessed he was an actor.

6. The hockey star had waved and had blown a kiss to the crowd.

7. "I do want love," Mrs. Ellis had stated.

8. "Do I want love?" Mrs. Ellis asked herself.

9. We have fished all week and have caught nothing.

10. The criminal had been found in a back yard with a bag full of money.

(Answers on page 108)

Exercise 7—Verbs

Using the dictionary as needed, find the missing verb forms in order to complete the following chart. There is no need to list an auxiliary verb.

Present Tense	Past Tense	Past Participle	Present Participle
1. laugh	_____	_____	_____
2. freeze	_____	_____	_____
3. _____	fell	_____	_____
4. _____	_____	drunk	_____
5. bring	_____	_____	_____
6. _____	_____	broken	_____
7. _____	shrank	_____	_____
8. _____	_____	_____	leading
9. _____	_____	swum	_____
10. write	_____	_____	_____

(Answers on page 109)

The ABCs of English Grammar

Conjunctions ———————————————

Definition

A conjunction is a part of speech used to join words or to connect parts of a sentence.

Examples:

a. Scott *and* Lindsay are coming. (Here the conjunction "and" joins the nouns "Scott" and "Lindsay.")

b. We will ask *when* we need food. (Here the conjunction "when" joins the two parts on either side of it.)

Coordinating Conjunctions

The first class of conjunctions is the coordinating conjunctions, which connect two or more words or sentence elements of equal importance or rank.

Examples:

a. Go *or* stay.

b. They fought on land *and* sea.

c. He is young, *but* he swims well.

The coordinating conjunctions should be memorized, especially as they are so few in comparison to the other class of conjunctions, the subordinating conjunctions (discussed in the next segment). Also, note that three of them rhyme: ***and, but, for, or, nor, yet, so***.

Subordinating Conjunctions

The second class of conjunctions is the subordinating conjunctions, which connect two or more words or sentence elements of unequal rank.

Examples:

a. She worked *until* it was dark. (The fact that she worked is a more important consideration than the fact that it was dark.)

b. She came *whenever* she could. (The fact that she came is the more important point.)

Common subordinating conjunctions are: *if, though, even though, although, rather than, as if, in order that, so that, when, whenever, while, how, where, because, that, until, whether, than, as, unless, since, before, after, even.*

Prepositions

Definition

A preposition is a word (for example, "on") or group of words (for example, "in order to") that connects a substantive (noun or pronoun) to some other element in the sentence; this connected substantive is known as the object of the preposition. Every preposition—without exception—has an object of the preposition, and this is how they may be distinguished from conjunctions.

Examples:

a. We spoke of her. (The preposition "of" connects the substantive "her" to the verb "spoke.")

b. Maria saw the light in the house. (The preposition "in" connects the substantive "house" to the substantive "light.")

c. The rose smelled good to him. (The preposition "to" connects the substantive "him" to the describing word, or adjective, "good." (See page 21.)

Exercise 8—Prepositions

In this exercise, write each sentence, draw a circle around the prepositions, and draw a rectangle around the objects of the preposition.

Example:

She sang (before) [breakfast].

1. It was hard for us.

2. He stood in front of the door and wouldn't let us enter the house.

3. We work during rain, hail, sleet or snow.

(Note that the object of the preposition may be compound, which means that there is more than one object for the same preposition.

4. Sukhpal lived on a farm when he was little.

5. She spoke to them.

6. He dropped his cigarette, then ran towards the bus stop.

7. She announced the news of the party, but nobody was interested.

8. The cup fell from the counter and broke.

9. He spoke concerning the question, but nobody understood him.

10. "I'll stay for a while," said her friend, hugging her.

   (Answers on page 109)

Exercise 9—Prepositions

In this exercise, there are rectangles around the objects of the preposition. Copy out each sentence. Circle the prepositions and underline the word or words which the prepositions connect to the objects of the preposition in each sentence.

Examples:

a. He saw <u>birds</u> (on) the [wires] . (Here "birds" should be underlined; the preposition "on" connects the substantive "birds" to the object of the preposition "wires."

b. They <u>sang</u> (from) the [platform]. (Here "sang" should be underlined; the preposition "from" connects the verb "sang" to the object of the preposition "platform.")

c. It felt <u>soft</u> and <u>tender</u> (to) [him]. (Here "soft" and "tender" should be underlined; the preposition "to" connects these describing words (adjectives) to the object of the preposition "him.")

1. Janet went to the [game].

2. The horse galloped across the [beach].

3. We loved the grin on his [face].

4. The car seems in fine [condition].

5. My father punished Jim for his [mistake].

6. He stood above [Tom].

7. Shane repaired the roof of the [house].

8. We saw the dog from the [pound].

9. Jane was kind to [Rochester].

10. The falcon swooped between the [trees].

(Answers on page 110)

Exercise 10—Prepositions

More than one preposition in a sentence may indicate that there is more than one object of the preposition.

Example:

She put the <u>lid</u> (on) the |can| and <u>went</u> (to) the |door| (with) |it|.

Here, there are three prepositions: the first connects a substantive to a substantive; the other two connect one verb to two substantives:

   i. <u>lid</u> on |can|

   ii. <u>went</u> to |door|

  iii. <u>went</u> with |it|

(Note that the prepositions "to" and "with" connect the same verb "went" to two different objects of the preposition.)

Instructions:

Write each sentence; then follow the examples:

   a. Circle the prepositions.

   b. Underline the word, or words, in each sentence that the preposition connects to the object or objects of the preposition.

   c. Draw a rectangle around each object of the preposition.

1. She went down the road and into the restaurant.

2. David threw the ball on the floor, and then he stepped on his cue and broke it.

3. Mr. Joe was beside the store when he saw an accident down the street.

4. You deserve the blue ribbon for that animal.

5. For that animal, you deserve the blue ribbon.

6. He jumped from the garage roof and landed on a sharp twig.

7. He is a violinist beyond expectation, and I have great hopes for him.

8. The man behind him saw the problem before the others.

9. In the ditch, covered with mud, the dwarf lay still.

10. He came through the operation and recovered within two weeks.

(Answers on page 110)

Review Exercises — Nouns, Pronouns, Verbs, Conjunctions and Prepositions

Exercise 11

Head five columns, each with one of the above parts of speech. Where possible, put the words in the following sentences into the correct column.

1. Jane ordered salmon with vegetables, and she asked for dessert.

2. They loved their boat because it gave them a chance at freedom.

3. "Frank will give you a pill in the morning," the man said.

4. Rani will call you when she needs them.

5. While he has been unwell, he shall attend the meeting.

6. Men, women, and children will come whenever they can because everyone loves excitement.

7. The relatives should arrive on Monday, and we hope they can come before dinner.

8. Although nobody had expected it, the city was covered in snow.

9. I will go, but I must return by the weekend.

10. The men left before Stephanie awoke, and she knew they were heading for trouble.

(Answers on page 111)

Exercise 12

Follow the instructions for Exercise 1.

1. Whenever it felt in the mood, the eagle would fly above the peak.

2. Put the tools beneath the bench until I have space for them in the cupboard.

3. Greg and Brett studied into the night because each of them was terrified of failure.

4. We searched under the snow, but couldn't find Jean-Paul.

5. I know the tree is an arbutus because it sheds its berries, leaves and bark.

6. During the year, we regularly climb the hill for exercise and stare at houses beyond the lake.

7. All will come unless they are caught in traffic.

8. Eat before you go if you can manage it.

9. While you were gone, Laurie Nordstrom came, but she said she would call you on the telephone.

10. We will play a game when Jim or Buck causes a problem.

(Answers on page 112)

Chapter 2

Parts of Speech
Part II

Adjectives

Definition

An adjective is a word that modifies or describes a noun or pronoun. Note italics in the three sets of examples.

Examples:

a. The *yellow* cockatoo screamed its displeasure. (The adjective "yellow" modifies, or describes, the noun "cockatoo.")

b. The boy is *angry*. (The adjective "angry" modifies, or describes, the noun "boy.")

Adjectives in the Positive Degree

Adjectives are in the positive degree when they describe a quality of a substantive (naming word).

Examples:

a. He is *short*. (The adjective "short" describes the pronoun "he.")

b. The *attractive* woman smiled. (The adjective "attractive" modifies the noun "woman.")

c. *This* book is a grammar text. ("This," as it is used here, is an adjective because it describes the noun "book." In another sentence, such as "I see this," "this" would be regarded as a pronoun.)

Adjectives in the Comparative Degree

The comparative degree of the adjective is used to compare or contrast two substantives. In regular adjectives, *–er* is usually added to the positive degree (*nice, nicer*). Some adjectives are irregular: the comparative of "good" is "better". Sometimes "more" is placed before the positive degree (*more happy*).

Examples:

a. Jamie was a *stronger* girl than Tess.

b. Her story was *more believable* than his.

Adjectives in the Superlative Degree

Superlative forms of the adjective are used to compare or contrast groups of three or more. The superlative form of regular adjectives is usually indicated by adding -st (*nice, nicest*) or –est (*sweet, sweetest*) to the positive form, or by placing the word "most" before the positive form.

Examples:

a. Lucille was the *smartest* person in the class.

b. It was the *most polluted* park he had seen.

IMPORTANT NOTE:

If there is any doubt about which adjective to use, especially when the adjective is irregular (does not follow the rules), look in the dictionary for the adjective in the positive degree. The adjectives in the comparative and superlative degrees will be listed as well.

Examples:

a. *good* (entry word in dictionary)

b. *better* (the irregular comparative adjective is listed second)

c. *best* (the irregular superlative adjective is listed last)

            The ABCs of English Grammar

Compound Adjectives

In compound adjectives, the hyphen is used between words that function as a single adjective before a substantive.

Examples:

a. She was an *on-the-ball* woman. (The woman was on the ball.)

b. It was a *first-rate* performance. (The performance was first rate.)

Exercise 13—Adjectives

On separate paper, write the number of each sentence and list the adjectives contained in each one.

1. The dog was a magnificent example of the breed.

2. The small, twisted man advanced towards me.

3. The wicked witch was not a pleasant person.

4. Mount Robson, shimmering, gleaming, soared above us.

5. My athletic uncle rode his ancient bicycle.

6. She gave a long, rambling, meaningless speech.

7. The spotted fawn stood silently within the green glade.

8. Her beloved son was coming home from a long weekend in the detox center (alternate spelling: centre).

9. Tired, desperate, he searched for his parents.

10. Those flowers in the garden are beautiful.

(Answers on page 114)

Exercise 14—Adjectives

Follow the instructions given in Exercise 1 on Adjectives.

1. The collie is different from the poodle.

2. Sarah is tall and blue-eyed.

3. The hat was made with this material.

4. She was a graceful dancer.

5. Are these condos yours?

6. "He is a rewarding boy in many ways," the grinning father said.

7. The large and the small houses belong to my greedy old aunt.

8. He rode ten miles on Thursday and twelve miles on Friday.

9. He won second prize in the long-distance race.

10. Each student bought the expensive equipment.

(Answers on page 114)

Adverbs

Definition

An adverb is a word used to describe or modify a verb, an adjective, or another adverb. It can also modify a participle. (A participle is classified as a verbal. See details of this on page 101.)

Examples:

a. He ran *quickly* to the house. (The adverb "quickly" modifies, or describes, the verb "ran.")

b. The girl had *very* dark hair. (Here, the adverb "very" modifies the adjective "dark.")

c. She talked *extremely* quickly. (Here, the the adverb "extremely" modifies the adverb "quickly.")

IMPORTANT NOTE:

"Not" and its contraction "n't" are always adverbs, so are **not** part of the simple predicate.

NOTE:

"Something" can be a noun or an adverb; "anything" can be a noun, pronoun, or adverb; "nothing" can be a noun or an adverb.

Adverbs in the Positive Degree

An adverb is regarded as being in the positive degree when it applies to only one thing or person.

Example:

Quietly, the engine turned. ("Quietly" describes the verb "turned" with regard to a single engine.)

Adverbs in the Comparative Degree

The comparative form of the adverb is used to compare or contrast two things or persons only. The comparative form of the adverb is most often formed by using "more" or "less" before the adverb.

Examples:

a. He argues *better* than Charles. (The adverb "better" compares the arguing of the two.)

b. Irene came *more recently* than Ian. (The adverbs "more" and "recently" both distinguish some difference in time between Irene's and Ian's visits.)

Adverbs in the Superlative Degree

The superlative form of the adverb is used to compare or contrast three or more things or persons. This form of the adverb most often uses "most" or "least" before the adverb.

Example:

Of all the members in the band, he marched the *most proudly*. (The adverbs "most proudly" show, in the superlative degree, how he marched.)

NOTE:

"Well" is always an adverb; "good" is always an adjective.

Exercise 15—Adverbs

On separate paper, write the number of each sentence and list the adverbs contained in each one.

1. He sang loudly in the back yard.

2. The Andersons arrived later than the Kwoks.

3. He played the game hard and well.

4. He had an extremely long pony tail.

5. The man drove very cautiously on the icy roads.

6. Wildly, lovingly, he hugged his horse.

7. The old lady spoke most kindly to the girl.

8. He visited once, but he never came again.

9. He recited marvellously, and his parents clapped happily when he had finished.

10. Apprehensively, he prepared himself for another round of verbal abuse.

(Answers on page 115)

The ABCs of English Grammar

Exercise 16—Adverbs

Follow the instructions given for Exercise 1 on Adverbs.

1. The girl was modestly dressed.

2. The hyena screamed shrilly, then viciously darted for its prey.

3. She ran particularly fast when we timed her.

4. Magic Johnson threw the basketball cleanly through the hoop.

5. He wrote a rather sad letter to his terminally ill father.

6. Extremely frightened, shaking uncontrollably, he sped to the side of his dearly loved parent.

7. The tortoise travelled more speedily on skates.

8. She performed exceptionally on the violin.

9. His behavior is somewhat better today.

10. My seriously ill wife called the doctor, and he said he would come immediately.

(Answers on page 115)

Articles ——————————

Definite Article

"The" is the only definite article; it points out a specific person, place, thing, or idea.

Indefinite Articles

"A" and "an" are both indefinite articles as they do not point out a specific person, place, thing, or idea. Use "a" before words starting with a consonant and "an" before words starting with a vowel.

Interjections

An interjection is an expression which indicates strong emotion. It may consist of more than one word, but it is short and ends with an exclamation mark.

Examples:

a. Ouch!

b. Cool!

c. Damn!

Exercise 17—Using All Parts of Speech

Every word in the following sentences can be placed into a part of speech category. As the exercise is challenging, please read the following instructions carefully.

1. Rewrite each sentence.

2. Underline all nouns once.

3. Underline all verbs twice.

4. Draw parentheses around adjectives. (*blue*)

5. Draw brackets around adverbs. [*fast*]

6. Draw a circle around pronouns.

7. Draw a "C" above conjunctions.

8. Draw a "P" above prepositions.

9. Draw an "A" above articles.

10. Draw an "I" above interjections.

1. "Aha!" exclaimed a smiling Sherlock Holmes. "I think now I understand!"

2. Quietly, the small girl entered the dusty room and put the plastic statue on the table.

3. He hasn't given me a thing; however, as I expected nothing, I was without disappointment.

4. Please tell them if anybody should come. (You might need to check your dictionary to find out about the word "please.")

5. The boys came later, and we were glad when they arrived.

6. He carefully placed the heavy book back in the lower drawer, then turned around.

7. All felt gloriously happy whenever they rode their bicycles.

8. Mrs. Conway neatly removed the leg of the turkey with the sharpened knife.

9. "I'm always happy when we're finished with winter and begin the glory of spring."

10. "This is a treat, Mrs. Moon," the smiling boy said as he happily raised his fork. "I never expected pie!"

(Answers on page 116)

Exercise 18—Using All Parts of Speech

Follow the same instructions given for Exercise 1 – Using All Parts of Speech.

1. He was a delightful baby and rarely cried at night.

2. Who pushed the colored pencil into the cracked wood of the ancient desk?

3. "Oh!" the startled girl exclaimed. "I am absolutely terrified of snakes!"

4. Whoever the woman was, she knew with certainty that the large family was in serious difficulty.

5. "Is somebody coming on Thursday, Mom?" the little girl asked eagerly.

6. We wandered aimlessly and didn't worry about it.

7. They sat down in the hope their lawyer would listen to their unbelievable story.

8. Each leaned quietly against the tree before he made his final decision.

9. "The parcel should have arrived last Thursday, shouldn't it?"

10. The loving father glowed happily as his young daughter went to the stage for her bronze medallion.

(Answers on page 117)

The ABCs of English Grammar

Chapter 3

Sentence Structure

Sentence Structure ────────────

Definition

A sentence is a group of words that begins with a capital letter and ends with a period, a question mark, or an exclamation mark. It must contain at least one independent clause. (See *Independent Clauses*, page 33.)

Example:

<u>Laurel</u> <u>ate</u> steak.

Because a sentence must contain a subject and a predicate and stand independently, the first requirement is to find the subject of the sentence by asking "**What** are we talking about?" or "**Who** are we talking about?" In this case, the answer to "**Who** are we talking about?" is "Laurel," and, therefore, "Laurel" serves as the subject of the sentence.

The predicate, which is always a verb, says or states something about the subject. In the above example, the simple predicate is "ate."

It is interesting how a sentence may have words added to it but still contain the one subject and the one predicate.

Examples:

a. <u>Laurel</u> <u>ate</u> steak.

b. Hungry <u>Laurel</u> greedily <u>ate</u> the delicious steak.

Here are a few more examples of sentences with their subjects underlined once and their predicates underlined twice.

c. <u>He</u> <u>enjoyed</u> the party. (<u>Who</u> are we talking about?)

d. The <u>party</u> <u>ended</u>. (<u>What</u> are we talking about?)

e. The horrendous <u>frog</u> <u>devoured</u> the insects. (<u>What</u> are we talking about?)

f. <u>I</u> <u>am</u> <u>enjoying</u> the party. (Note that the auxiliary verb and the main verb, side by side, are regarded as one predicate.)

g. <u>Jack</u> and <u>Karen</u> <u>went</u>. (Here there are two subjects for the same verb—commonly called a compound subject.)

IMPORTANT NOTE:

All pronouns used as subjects must be in the subjective case (*I, you, he, she, we, they, who*). The subjective case indicates a noun or pronoun in a sentence about which something is said in the predicate.

Example:

<u>Me</u> is hungry. (Incorrect)

<u>I</u> am hungry. (Correct)

Clauses ──────────────────

Definition

A clause is a group of related words containing a subject and a predicate. There can be more than one clause in a sentence.

Independent Clauses

An independent (sometimes called "main," or "principal") clause is named for the fact that, with its subject and predicate, it can stand alone as an independent sentence. In the examples, the subjects are underlined once; the predicates twice.

Examples:

a. The <u>girl</u> <u>skied</u>.

b. The <u>mayor</u> <u>lost</u> the election.

c. <u>You</u> <u>have</u> <u>seen</u> him?

d. <u>Have</u> <u>you</u> <u>seen</u> him? (Notice that in a question the subject can be placed between the auxiliary and the main verbs.)

Two independent clauses may be connected with a comma plus a coordinating conjunction, or with a semicolon placed between the independent clauses. (See page 13, if necessary, to review coordinating conjunctions.)

Examples:

a. (The <u>family</u> <u>came</u>), and (<u>they</u> <u>stayed</u>.)

b. (The <u>family</u> <u>came</u>); (<u>they</u> <u>stayed</u>.)

The difference in punctuation may indicate a different emphasis in the relationship between the clauses.

IMPORTANT NOTE:
If a coordinating conjunction introduces the clause, it is not regarded as part of the clause.

Dependent Clauses

A dependent (or subordinate) clause, like all clauses, has a subject and a predicate, but cannot stand alone as a separate, or independent, sentence.

Example:

     DC   IC

(If <u>we</u> <u>had</u> <u>gone</u>), (<u>we</u> <u>would</u> <u>have</u> <u>got</u> money.)

The dependent clause (DC), "if we had gone," has a subject, "we," and a predicate, "had gone"; however, if this clause stood alone, the reader or listener would be waiting for something else to complete the thought. The independent clause (IC), "we would have got money," allows that completion.

A dependent clause may be introduced by a subordinating conjunction. (See pages 13 and 14, if necessary, to review subordinating conjunctions.)

Examples:

IC   DC

a. (He came) (whenever I came.)

        DC   IC

b. (Because I came), (he came.)

IMPORTANT NOTE:

Most of the time, there is no comma separating the clauses when an independent clause comes before a dependent clause. However, if the independent clause makes a statement, and the dependent clause explains why, you must decide if it would be better for a reader to pause. If so, the clauses should be separated with a comma.

Examples:

a. He stayed because the party was over.

                         or

    He stayed, because the party was over.

b. We will not see him as he has gone.

                         or

    We will not see him, as he has gone.

(Probably, as in the second sentence of both examples, a comma is appropriate.)

There may be more than one subordinating conjunction to introduce a dependent clause.

Examples:

a. He can come no matter how I hate him.

b. Inasmuch as he was wrong, I forgive him.

A dependent clause may be introduced by a relative pronoun. (See page 5.)

Examples:

IC   (rp) DC

a. My <u>book</u> <u>is</u> one that <u>I</u> <u>like</u>.

IC   (rp) DC

b. <u>I</u> <u>know</u> that <u>you</u> <u>are</u>.

A relative pronoun may be omitted but understood.

Examples:

IC   rp DC

a. (<u>This</u> <u>is</u> the store) [that] (<u>we</u> <u>know</u>.)

IC   rp   DC

b. (<u>I</u> <u>remember</u> the day) [when] <u>I</u> last <u>saw</u> her.)

Basically, a dependent clause functions as an adverb, an adjective, or a noun.

Examples:

a. Throw the ball <u>as hard as you can</u>.
   (dependent clause functions as an adverb)

b. There are streets <u>where I live</u>.
   (dependent clause functions as an adjective)

c. Here are three examples of dependent clauses functioning as nouns:

   i. <u>Whatever you think</u> could be a lie.
      (a dependent clause used as a subject—see page 74)

   ii. I do not know <u>what's on his mind</u>.
       (a dependent clause used as a direct object—see page 77)

   iii. Give the money to <u>whomever wants it</u>.
        (a dependent clause used as an object of the preposition—see pages 75 and 76)

Basic Points to Remember

With regard to dependent and independent clauses, the basic points to remember are:

1. Every clause must have a subject and a predicate. Sometimes, only a predicate is shown as in the command, "<u>Go</u>!" In such a case, the subject is "you" which, neither written nor said, is understood to mean "<u>You go</u>!")

2. All sentences must have at least one independent clause in order to function independently.

3. Two independent clauses, or two dependent clauses, may be separated with a comma plus a coordinating conjunction (a reminder that a coordinating conjunction introducing a clause is not part of that clause) or with a semicolon.

4. If a dependent clause comes before an independent clause, there should be a comma separating them.

5. Remember there can be two subjects (a compound subject) or two predicates (a compound predicate), or both, in a single clause.

Example:

<u>Chen Ji</u> and <u>John</u> <u>laughed</u> and <u>danced</u>.

Restrictive Relative Clauses

The restrictive relative clause (sometimes called an identifying clause) identifies the substantive it describes. It is not set off with commas. In the following examples, the restrictive relative clauses are underlined.

Examples:

a. Matt hates grammar <u>that isn't clear</u>.
   (Here the substantive described is "grammar.")

b That's the boy <u>who brings presents to Anna</u>.
   (Here the substantive described is "boy.")

Nonrestrictive Relative Clauses

A nonrestrictive relative clause (underlined in the example) is unnecessary to identify the substantive it describes and is set off with commas.

Example:

Matt, <u>who loves peaches</u>, likes girls.

NOTE:
The nonrestrictive relative clause can usually be omitted when the relative pronoun is immediately followed by a form of the verb "to be" (*is, are, was, were*, for example).

Example:

Melanie (who was exhausted) dragged herself home.

Exercise 19—Clauses

On separate paper, write out each of the following sentences and then:

1. Underline the subjects once.

2. Underline the predicates twice.

3. Draw parentheses around each dependent and independent clause.

4. Label each clause to indicate whether it is an independent (**IC**) or dependent (**DC**) clause.

5. Insert any missing punctuation.

Here are a couple of examples as to how to complete the exercise:

        IC   DC

a. (<u>John</u> <u>arrived</u>) (as <u>I</u> <u>was</u> <u>leaving</u>.)

        DC   IC

b. (As <u>I</u> <u>was</u> <u>leaving</u>), (<u>John</u> <u>arrived</u>.)

1. He wrote a novel and it was wild.

2. The parcel came when I was away.

3. While she waited she set the VCR.

4. I hate it whenever you spit on me.

5. We know the artist his name is Georges Costaz.

6. Before she put the tent up the storm began.

7. The men recognized the thief who had stolen their money.

8. Mr. Jackson participated although he has regretted it since. (Remember auxiliary and main verbs.)

9. Whenever he can Joe swings with the crowd.

10. Because you said it I will believe it.

(Answers on page 118)

Exercise 20—Clauses

Some of the following sentences contain compound subjects and predicates. With this in mind complete this exercise following the same instructions given in Exercise 1 on Clauses.

1. Won-bin and Chi-woong go whenever they can.

2. The whole family studies clams and oysters.

3. Before Elizabeth arrived Mother and Dad had prepared her room.

4. The man and his wife have sold their house.

5. When our friends visited we played bridge.

6. Both boys and girls cooked and cleaned.

7. He was unhappy after you jumped insanely on his car hood last week.

8. Unless he has an accident, Harry will be going.

9. While he was thinking about the problem he was distracted by a sting on his neck.

10. Since you and Rita went to Toronto Jane and I have missed you.

(Answers on page 118)

Exercise 21—Clauses

For this exercise the instructions are the same as for Exercises 1 and 2; however, here there are three or more clauses, so the punctuation will require particular attention.

1. While they were there they enjoyed the people and they loved the climate.

2. Mr. Pai asked the man when the train arrived but he received no definite answer.

3. Our groups stayed together and we all went to the beach whenever we could.

4. Have you seen her or have you seen Bix since we last met?

5. Because I am familiar with him I recommend him and I think you will like him.

6. She does know Simmer I know Susan and we both know Shing.

7. Whenever Sam gets a job he keeps it only two or three days before he loses it.

8. They will look for the treasure after they have located the map they received in the mail.

9. I remember when I last saw her for it was my birthday.

10. Whenever he yells the children and dogs run until they can hear him no longer.

(Answers on page 119)

The ABCs of English Grammar

Sentences Classified by Structure ——

When considering "sentences classified by structure," the basic concern is the kind of clause, or clauses, involved (IC or DC) and the number of clauses being considered.

Simple Sentences

The simple sentence consists of one independent clause.

Examples:

a. The <u>couple</u> <u>fought</u> nonstop.

b. Terrified, the <u>boy</u> <u>fainted</u>.

There can be words added to describe the subject and/or words added to describe the predicate, but the sentence remains simple with the one independent clause.

Examples:

a. The joyously happy <u>couple</u> <u>played</u> catch with a frozen fish.

b. The excited <u>girl</u> <u>bought</u> the gorgeous, blue bicycle.

Compound Sentences

The compound sentence consists of two or more independent clauses.

NOTE: All examples of clauses are enclosed in parentheses.

Examples:

a. (He <u>came</u>); (he <u>saw</u>); (he <u>conquered</u>).

b. (He <u>came</u>), and (he <u>saw</u>), and (he <u>conquered</u>).

c. (I <u>liked</u> her), for (<u>she</u> <u>was</u> nice to me).

Complex Sentences

The complex sentence contains only one independent clause and one or more dependent clauses. The independent clause may be before or after a dependent clause.

Examples:

a. (When <u>Anne</u> <u>came</u> to my house), (<u>we</u> <u>had</u> fun).
(1 DC + comma + 1 IC)

b. (<u>We</u> <u>had</u> fun) (when <u>Anne</u> <u>came</u> to my house).
(1 IC + 1 DC)

c. (Although <u>I</u> <u>understand</u> clauses), (<u>I</u> <u>have</u> <u>had</u> little practice)(because our <u>class</u> <u>hasn't</u> <u>done</u> any exercises on them).
(1 DC + comma + 1 IC + 1 DC)

d. (When <u>I</u> <u>understand</u> clauses), and (when <u>I</u> <u>can</u> <u>punctuate</u> properly), (my <u>grades</u> <u>will</u> <u>improve</u>).
(1 DC + comma + coordinating conjunction + 1 DC + comma + 1 IC)

IMPORTANT NOTE:
Remember, the coordinating conjunctions such as "and," which may introduce a clause, are not regarded as part of that clause.

Compound-Complex Sentences

The compound-complex sentence contains two or more independent clauses and one or more dependent clauses.

Examples:

a. (The <u>scientist</u> <u>knew</u>) (his <u>experiment</u> <u>was</u> a success), but (<u>he</u> <u>said</u> nothing) (until <u>he</u> <u>had</u> <u>finished</u> his drink.)
(IC + DC + comma + coordinating conjunction + IC + DC. The second clause is dependent because the relative pronoun "that" is omitted, but understood.)

b. <u>Noor</u> <u>likes</u> sushi), and (when <u>she</u> <u>gets</u> the chance), (<u>she</u> <u>eats</u> it.
   (IC + comma + coordinating conjunction + DC + comma + IC)

c. (<u>He</u> <u>is</u> <u>going</u>), so (<u>do</u> <u>you</u> <u>think</u> (<u>you</u> <u>will</u> <u>go</u>)?
   (IC + comma + coordinating conjunction + IC + DC)

Exercise 22—The Four Basic Types of Sentences

Review the material on the four basic types of sentences, then write each of the sentences in this exercise on separate paper. Follow the instructions below to complete the exercise.

1. Underline the subjects once.

2. Underline the predicates twice.

3. Draw parentheses around and label the independent clauses with IC.*

4. Draw parentheses around and label the dependent clauses with DC.*

5. Insert any missing punctuation.

6. State at the end of the sentence whether the sentence is simple, compound, complex, or compound-complex.

* See the examples on pages 34-36.

1. We met whenever we could.

2. Celine Dion delivered a fantastic performance.

3. Wherever he goes my thoughts will not be with him.

4. We should have gone on the cruise and I wish we had.

5. When we saw the delightful puppy we couldn't resist her.

6. "Give me my money now!"

7. He will come or I will drag him here.

8. Bert said the man was handsome and smart but I could never love a wimp. (Before you make a decision on what type of sentence this is, recall that a relative pronoun may be omitted but understood. See the second set of examples on page 36.)

9. Although I loved the motorcycle I sold it because I feared I would have another accident. (See the comment in parentheses for Q. 8.)

10. Until he saw the photograph of himself, he hadn't realized that he had bowed legs.

(Answers on page 120)

Chapter 4

Sentence Tones

Sentence Tones

Definition

"Sentence tones" is a title to indicate that there is a tone, or mood, in a sentence that one person tries to communicate to another.

Basically, with "sentence tones," sentences are classified according to their function, or use.

Declarative Sentence

A declarative sentence makes a statement of some kind.

Examples:

a. He has a face covered with zits.

b. I shot the moose in the left nostril.

c. Barbra Streisand won an Academy Award when she was in her twenties.

Exclamatory Sentence

An exclamatory sentence expresses strong or sudden emotion or feeling. It usually ends with an exclamation mark.

Examples:

a. Someone has stolen my credit card!

b. There's no dog as good as the pit bull!

c. "You're no friend of mine, you jelly-brained scum!" he exclaimed.

NOTE:
Don't overuse the exclamatory sentence, especially in formal writing, because it tends to make a writer seem overly emotional.

Imperative Sentence

An imperative sentence consists of a command, a request, or an earnest request.

Examples:

a. You take charge of the firing squad. (command)

b. I ask that everybody stand and bow in my direction. (request)

c. Give me the strength for the job that I must do. (earnest request)

NOTE #1: The pronoun "you" may be the subject in an imperative sentence.

Examples:

a. You take the bubble gum.

b. You wear your raincoat.

NOTE #2: Sometimes, the subject "you" is understood rather than said or written.

Examples:

a. (you) Take the bubble gum.

b. (you) Wear your raincoat.

NOTE #3: Occasionally, an exclamation mark may be used for emphasis in an imperative sentence.

Examples:

a. Let's go!

b. You must not lose your wallet!

Interrogative Sentence

An interrogative sentence asks a question.

Examples:

a. Are you an elf?

b. Can you visit more than once a day?

c. Which is your favorite game?

Exercise 23—Sentence Tones

Read the following sentences. On a separate piece of paper, decide whether each is declarative, exclamatory, imperative, or interrogative; also, write the ending punctuation that would be necessary. Note that there can be some variation in ending punctuation: "You are a fool in my arms!" would be exclamatory, while "You are a fool in my arms." would be declarative. Also note that quotation marks, which will be covered in Chapter 5, are omitted.

1. All of us must leave at once

2. I've lived in this city all my life

3. Is your name Ian, or idiot

4. What an advantage my calculator is to me

5. Good Lord, are you having blackouts again

6. My youngest son is the result of in vitro fertilization

7. I heard you were buried alive by a mud slide

8. You deserve the blue ribbon for that wonderful animal

9. I am sorry to report that you did an unsatisfactory job of repairing the toilet

10. Please leave us alone

(Answers on page 121)

Chapter 5

Punctuation

The Period

1. The period is properly placed at the end of a declarative or an imperative sentence.

Examples:

a. Deer like to browse. (declarative sentence)

b. Please return to your seat. (imperative sentence)

2. The period is also used for upper case (capital letter) abbreviations.

Examples:

a. N. (or N) may be used for north; NW. (or NW) for northwest. Note that points of the compass are not capitalized when used for directions but are capitalized when used for geographic terms such as *Western Canada, Far East, North Pole.*)

b. A.D. (anno Domini—the years since the beginning of the Christian era)

c. E.S.T. (eastern standard time)

3. Periods are used for lower case (small letter) abbreviations as well as for abbreviations which have a beginning upper case letter followed by small case letters.

Examples:

a. a.m. (antemeridian—before noon—may be written by hand as A.M.)

b. m.p.h. (miles per hour) or mph

c. Ont. (But use the two-letter standardized postal forms such as ON [Ontario] and NV [Nevada] when addressing mail.)

d. Mr. (Mister); Mrs. (title of a married woman); Ms. (title of a woman who may be married or single); Miss (used for girls; single women; married women who retain their birth name for professional purposes)

4. Periods are used with the initials of people and with the abbreviation of titles or degrees.

Note that periods are not generally used for abbreviations of organizations and are not used after metric measurements.

Examples:

a. George G. Jones

b. B.A. (Bachelor of Arts)

c. CBS, YMCA, NHL

d. The speed limit is 110 km/h. (Note that the style is different from mph.)

IMPORTANT NOTE:
If a sentence ends in an abbreviation using a period, a second period is not necessary.

5. A period may be used to end footnotes (a note or reference at the bottom of a page which refers to a book or reference used in the writing of material).

Example:

McCarthy, Cormac (1995). *All the Pretty Horses*. New York: Vintage Books.

NOTE: This is only one of the many styles of reference.

6. The period is used to mark a decimal.

Examples:

a. I paid $ 3.52 for the gift.

b. The price of my house has increased by 40.3%.

The Comma

1. The comma is used before and after words of direct address.

Examples:

a. Yes, young man, you may go.

b. Jeanne, you did well on that test.

2. As indicated on page 34, a comma followed by a coordinating conjunction may separate two independent clauses. If you haven't done so, it would be a good idea to memorize the coordinating conjunctions: *and, but, for, nor, or, yet, so.*

Examples:

a. He came, and I came.

b. Either you go, or I will.

3. A comma may be used to separate coordinate adjectives— adjectives of equal rank which come before the noun they modify.

Example:

He was a young, healthy man. (Here both *young* and *healthy* modify or describe, *man*. Note that *and* could replace the comma.)

4. A comma is used to separate a dependent clause from an independent clause that follows it, or to separate a phrase which precedes an independent clause. (Phrases will be detailed in Chapter 6. Basically, what it is necessary to realize is that a phrase may contain **either** a subject **or** a predicate, or it may contain **neither** a subject **nor** a predicate.)

Examples:

a. Whatever you say, I won't marry you. (The dependent clause precedes the independent clause.)

b. Time after time, he tried to train the dog to urinate and excrete on paper. (Here the comma separates the phrase "Time after time" from the independent clause which follows.)

5. Commas may be used to separate interrupters, or words that aren't really necessary for sentence meaning.

Examples:

a. Yes, I think you are skinny.

b. I think you are skinny, yes.

6. Unless they end the sentence, the abbreviations for academic degrees, and titles that follow a name, should have a comma after them.

Example:

Dr. F. Maxim, M.D., gave the speech.

7. Commas may be used to separate three or more words, phrases, or clauses.

Examples:

a. I'm crazy about *hippopotamuses, octopuses, porpoises, dolphins* and *blue whales*. (Here the commas separate a series of substantives. Note that there isn't a comma before the "and.")

b. *By the river, near the fence, at the mimosa tree,* I declared my love. (Here there are three phrases, each set off with commas, before the independent clause, "I declared my love.")

   c. *He was poor, he was hungry, he was dirty.* (Here there is a series of clauses, each one of them separated from the others by a comma.)

8. Commas are used to separate nonrestrictive modifiers which are placed within the sentence. A nonrestrictive modifier gives additional information about the noun it modifies, but is not necessary to identify or define that noun.

Examples:

   a. Charlie Bear, a lonely man, won the lottery. (The quality of being lonely has nothing to do with winning or losing a lottery.)

   b. Her husband, whose former wife was a mechanic, will undergo surgery on his tongue tomorrow. (In this case, the former wife's job is not the main interest.)

9. The comma is used to set off a short, direct quotation whether it comes before or after the rest of the sentence.

Examples:

   a. She screamed, "Get out of my sight!"

   b. "You must never ask me to go on a roller coaster," she told him.

10. The comma is used to separate dates, addresses, geographical names and—an option—numbers more than four digits long.

Examples:

a. He was born on February 29, 1992. (Note: if the day of the month is not given [March 2003], or if the day of the month precedes rather than follows the month [4 March 2003], the commas may be omitted.)

b. She lives at 3107 Main Street, Everett, Washington, U. S. A. 29866 (Note: postal codes are not preceded by a comma.)

c. 18,690

11. Use a comma after the salutation of a friendly letter.

Examples:

a. Dear Moshe,

b. Dear friend, (Note that "friend" would not have a capital letter as it is not a proper noun.)

12. Commas are sometimes needed for clarity.

Example:

You could, could you?

The Semicolon

A semicolon allows a pause that is less than a period but longer than a comma. The semicolon can make it easier for the reader to understand the content of a long sentence.

Examples:

a. He ate; he drank; he left. (Here the semicolons are used to separate independent clauses not joined by a comma plus a coordinating conjunction.)

b. Devahi liked running, gymnastics, studying and working with her computer during the week; however, on the weekends, she liked to relax.

IMPORTANT NOTE:
As indicated in Example b, when words such as *therefore, however, nevertheless, accordingly, thus, then, hence* (called connective or conjunctive adverbs) separate two independent clauses, the semicolon comes before the connective adverb.

c. Sam got peas, carrots and squash from the grocer; tarts, doughnuts and pies from the baker; steak, chops and ribs from the butcher. (Here the semicolons are used to separate one series of items from another series when one of the items in a series has a comma after it.)

The Colon

The colon is used to introduce a formal statement, question, or quotation, to introduce some kind of list, after the salutation of a formal business letter, and it is also used between the parts of a number denoting time.

Examples:
a. Mr. Harding stood up and spoke: "To greet you all at this particular event gives me no pleasure." (The colon prepares the reader for the quoted statement.)

b. She borrowed what she needed for her skiing trip: skis, a warm, waterproof jacket, insulated mitts. (Here the colon introduces the list to follow.)

c. Dear Madam: (This is after the salutation of a business letter. Today, current practice in business letters is less formal and may omit a salutation.)

d. The time is 6:12 a.m.

NOTE:
The colon may also be used to show proportions (2:3); to separate a title and a sub-title; between city and publisher in bibliographies; to separate chapter and verse in Biblical citations.

The Exclamation Mark ———————

The exclamation mark is used after words or sentences that show strong emotion or feeling.

Examples:

a. Help!

b. You are an overbearing swine!

The Question Mark ———————

The question mark is placed at the end of every direct question and is also used parenthetically to express doubt.

Examples:

a. How much money do you make?

b. Jesus Christ, born in 4 B.C. (?), was a huge influence on many people.

The Hyphen

The hyphen is used between words which function as a single adjective unit; to separate the syllables of a word if part of the word is carried to the next line; in compound numbers from twenty-one to ninety-nine; for fractions used as words; to connect elements when the collision of two vowels would be awkward; with some prefixes such as anti-, post-, non-, over-; to indicate the omission of letters or words.

Examples:

a. It was a hard-to-find item. (The term "hard-to-find" functions as a single adjective which describes "item.")

b. Bobby was a pleasant dog who was very af-fec-tionate. (The word "affectionate" might have to be hyphenated between two of the syllables due to the fact that a portion of the word might need to go on a second line. The entry words in a dictionary, whether with dots, dashes, or some other symbol, will indicate how words must be syllabicated. A one-syllable word should never be hyphenated.)

c. forty-one, fifty-two, one-third, eighty-seven

d. semi-independent, re-educate

e. anti-Americanism, non-British

f. He is in deep s---. (The letters that follow "s" are known or guessed.)

The Dash

The dash may be used singly or in pairs to indicate an unexpected or abrupt change of thought; before a summarizing or concluding statement; to indicate an afterthought; to separate a list or series from the rest of the sentence; to attribute a quotation.

Examples:

a. "I was going to buy—where on earth is my child?—a sweater."

b. He planned, he practiced, he saved—all in preparation for surviving a year in India by playing the ukulele.

c. He gave me a—I'm sorry, I promised not to tell.

d. The great writers—Dante, Shakespeare, Tolstoi—will always be remembered.

e. "No boobies, no rubies."—Eva Gabor

IMPORTANT NOTE:
Don't overuse the dash or use it as a substitute for other punctuation.

The Apostrophe

The apostrophe is used to form the possessive case of: a) nouns not ending in "s"; b) plural nouns ending in "s"; c) indefinite pronouns; d) certain plural forms; e) the omission of one or more letters or figures.

Examples:

a. Jerry's foot (There is one person, so the apostrophe is placed before the *s*.)

b. women's dresses (The dresses belong to more than one woman. "Women," like "men," or "children," is a collective noun and takes the possessive apostrophe in the same way as a singular noun.)

c. the ladies' clothing (clothing that belongs to more than one lady); the dogs' kennels (kennels for more than one dog)

d. He is everyone's friend. She is somebody's daughter. (The reader doesn't know who "everybody" or "somebody" is, so these two words are examples of the possessive case of singular, indefinite pronouns.)

e. She drew three x's and then drew seven o's. Mind your p's and q's.

f. He was born in the '80s. (meaning the 1980s)

g. "The 'gator is dange'us, an' I can't go no closer," said the little boy. (Obviously, there are letters missing in the first three words with apostrophes. In the contraction "can't," the apostrophe stands for the missing letters "n" and "o.")

h. It's good. (The contraction "it's" **always** stands for "it is," and an apostrophe would never be used in a possessive such as "its" in "its nest." Possessive pronouns (*mine, yours, his, hers, its, ours, theirs*) never require apostrophes.

Quotation Marks – Double

Double quotation marks are used to enclose exact words spoken or written by another person (referred to as a direct quotation), and to indicate the titles of poems, songs, short stories, magazine articles, a chapter in a book, essays, titles of episodes of a television series, and musical works. Note that periods and commas are always placed inside the quotation marks.

Example:

a. He said, "Pollution should be of concern to all North Americans."

NOTE:

The above example a is a **direct quotation**. The utterance written as an **indirect quotation** would be: He said that pollution should be of concern to all North Americans.

b. "No," she replied, "we can never be married." (The sentence quoted must be enclosed in quotation marks. Note that the second part of the quoted sentence begins with a lower case letter.)

c. "Linda can never be married," he replied.

d. The girls sang the song "Unforgettable."

e. "Ozymandias" is his favorite poem.

f. "Running Wild" was the best segment of that television series.

g. Bach's "Little Fugue in G Minor" is my favorite.

NOTE:

A colon or a semicolon is always placed after the close-quotation marks (the second set) if it isn't part of the quotation.

Example:

He says he's a "free thinker"; what he might mean by this is scary to contemplate.

Quotation Marks – Single

Single quotation marks are used within double quotation marks for a quotation within a quotation.

Examples:

a. "Jennifer said, 'I'm going to make trouble,'" Sara told her mother.

b. "Julius Caesar said, '<u>Veni</u>, <u>vedi</u>, <u>vici</u>,' didn't he?" Bob Jones asked the teacher.
   (word processor option: *veni, vedi, vici*)

IMPORTANT NOTE:

An exclamation mark or a question mark goes inside the close-quotation marks if it is part of the quotation; if it isn't, it is placed outside the close-quotation marks.

Examples:

a. The student asked, "Are you sure of the exam date?"

b. I hate the song "Stairway to Heaven"!

✳ c. "Did George say, 'Come on Sunday'?"

NOTE:

Unless you're writing dialogue, try not to use too many quotation marks as it tends to look messy. The use of italics is a potential alternative.

Underlining

Underlining in a manuscript represents printed italics which should be used for the titles of books, newspapers, magazines, plays, operas, movies, television series, foreign words not assimilated into the English language (see first example b, page 62) and to emphasize words. Some publications italicize works of art, ships, trains, planes, but this practice is infrequent. If you used a word processsor, all of the underlining in the following examples could be replaced with italic type. (But if you are under the direction of a teacher and use a word processor, it would be wise to check with your instructor to learn which style he/she prefers.)

Examples:

a. I read <u>Open Secrets</u> by Alice Munro.
   or
   I read *Open Secrets* by Alice Munro.

b. He reads <u>The New York Times</u> on week-ends.

c. She reads <u>Sports Illustrated</u>.

d. "Have you seen the musical, <u>Grease</u>?"

e. Her favorite dramatic opera is <u>La Traviata</u>.

f. <u>Titanic</u> is her favorite movie.

g. <u>Seinfeld</u> was a unique television show.

h. One of William Shakespeare's best plays is <u>Julius Caesar</u>.

i. <u>Love</u> is a word that can be described in many ways.

Parentheses

Parentheses refers to the upright curved lines which may be used to insert definitions, incidental or additional information, illustrative detail, to enclose reference numbers or letters, and footnotes. If you use parentheses for afterthoughts, use them sparingly.

Examples:

a. I love the nuts of the grugru (a West Indian tree).

b. Quentin Tarantino, the film director (who often focuses on the seedier aspects of life), has won several awards for his work.

c. This household has three "don't" rules: (1) don't leave clothes on the floor; (2) don't leave dead skin and dirt in the bathtub; (3) don't throw food.

d. Roger's comment (p. 7) about loving the child while disliking his or her behavior is a good one.

e. James Redfield, *The Celestine Prophecy* (New York: Warner Books, Inc., 1993)

Ellipsis

Ellipsis consists of spaced periods used to indicate the omission of a word or words needed to complete a sentence or the omission of part of a quotation. Three spaced periods are used unless the ellipsis comes at the end of a sentence in the original, in which case a fourth period is used.

Examples:

a. The bill...passed.

b. I wanted to do it, but....

Exercise 24—Punctuation

Rewrite each of the following sentences with the required punctuation. Remember that the ending quotation marks must come **after** a period, question mark, or exclamation mark, not above it. (For example, "I love candy!")

1. Go away Harry the boy said

2. Susan do you believe Im a mentally challenged person her mother asked

3. Whenever Mr Fraley eats figs he gets diarrhea

4. He can go but you cant

5. Let me think no I dont think I can think Mrs Jones admitted

6. Everyone was shocked when the woman said thousands of animals a month are killed for medical research (Make this a direct quotation, although you could simply end it with a period, making it an indirect quotation.)

7. Beyond the fence past the bridge through the meadow I continued to walk towards town

8. Nancy Taylor who was once a dancer earned a medical degree

9. The dog was short fat adorable and incontinent

10. Adrian Felton lives at 2605 King Edward Street in Vancouver British Columbia

(Answers on page 122)

Exercise 25—Punctuation

Follow the instructions for Exercise 1.

1. You think I wouldn't do that she asked as she laughed in his miserable face

2. In January 1972 East Pakistan became the Republic of Bangladesh

3. Are you saying you have cheated the teacher asked go to the principals office now

4. He has gone back to the mountains the man said and I am going back too

5. Maurice Greene from Granada Hills California ran the 100 meter race in a record 9.79 seconds

6. Huge black frothing the enraged bull managed to gore my right thigh with his left horn

7. Mr Yates if you want my opinion is a loud-mouthed pain in the butt

8. She went so I went but I was sorry and so was she

9. She wrote Barbara G Smith MD at the bottom of the prescription

10. Travelling at 80 mph he finally stopped to set his watch to Mountain Standard Time

(Answers on page 123)

Exercise 26—Punctuation

Again, follow the instructions for Exercise 1 to complete this exercise.

1. This is a good idea and Antonio agrees

2. John F. Kennedy was assassinated on November 22 1963

3. He travelled 80 kph through the slums of Halifax Nova Scotia

4. Well Pierre the man said I think we should leave no later than 640 pm

The ABCs of English Grammar

5. Go back to your own house the man yelled at the dog do I have to kick you

6. Get out of my sight you pathetic piece of trash the secretary told the computer expert

7. Star Wars was a movie released exactly forty years after Snow White and the Seven Dwarfs

8. If you decide to stay at this camp there are four rules dont leave the camp without permission always travel with a buddy be on time for meals clean up your cabin

9. I love peaches pears and apples

10. Did Molly say please come on Thursday Julia asked I just cant remember

(Answers on page 123)

Chapter 6

Phrases

Definition

A phrase is a group of two or more grammatically related words functioning as a single part of speech. A phrase never contains both a subject and a predicate; it may contain neither a subject nor a predicate. (See pages 32 and 74 for a discussion of subject and predicate.) There are several types of phrases.

Noun Phrase

In a noun phrase, the whole phrase does the work of a noun.

Example:

Playing ball is fun. (Here the noun phrase operates as the subject because in answer to the subject-finding question, "**Who** are we talking about?" or "**What** are we talking about?" the answer is "playing ball." "Playing" is a gerund, which is explained on page 100.)

Verb Phrase

A verb phrase consists of the main verb and the one or more auxiliary verbs which precede it.

Examples:

a. She should be laughing. (The auxiliary verbs are "should" and "be"; the main verb is "laughing.")

b. He will have gone by Thursday. (The auxiliary verbs are "will" and "have"; the main verb is "gone.")

IMPORTANT NOTE:
"Not" or its contraction "n't" when included in the verb phrase is regarded as part of the verb phrase.

Adjective Phrase

An adjective phrase (sometimes called an adjectival phrase) modifies a substantive.

Examples:

a. The girls <u>on the boulevard</u> are models. (Here the adjective phrase "on the boulevard" describes, or modifies, the noun "girls." This phrase could also be regarded as a prepositional phrase because its leading word is a preposition.)

b. <u>Trying to twist her face into a smile</u>, she began to answer the man. (Here the whole adjective phrase modifies the pronoun "she." Note that part of this adjective phrase consists of a prepositional phrase: "into a smile.")

Also, because the key word in this phrase is "trying," the phrase may also be called a participial phrase. (There are details on participles on page 101.)

IMPORTANT NOTE:
If the adjective phrase begins the sentence, it must describe the subject of the sentence; also, it must be set off from the rest of the sentence with a comma, as indicated in Example b above.

Adverb Phrase

An adverb phrase modifies a verb.

Examples:

a. We lived <u>beyond the park</u>. (The adverb phrase "beyond the park" modifies, or describes, the verb "lived." This phrase could be regarded also as a prepositional phrase because its leading word is a preposition.)

b. <u>Without delay</u>, Gorbachev signed the documents declaring the U.S.S.R. an extinct nation. (The underlined words tell how Gorbachev signed the documents and thus makes up an adverb phrase modifying the verb "signed." As in the first example, this phrase, too, could be regarded as a prepositional phrase because it begins with a preposition. (See the following segment.)

Prepositional Phrase

All phrases that begin with a preposition, whether adjective or adverb phrases, may be regarded as prepositional phrases.

Example:

He will speak to her in the morning. (Both "to her" and "in the morning" are prepositional phrases as each begins with a preposition.)

Exercise 27—Phrases

On separate paper, list each of the underlined phrases and define each as noun, verb, adjective, or adverb. For this exercise, regard all prepositional phrases as either adjective or adverb phrases.

1. He went <u>in the morning</u>.

2. <u>The boy</u> <u>had seen</u> him yesterday.

3. <u>Raising her fist</u>, <u>the angry girl</u> turned <u>towards the boy</u>.

4. He chewed <u>a delicious Granny Smith apple</u>.

5. <u>That book</u> <u>on the desk</u> is mine.

6. <u>The buffalo</u> tramped <u>through the mud</u>.

7. They <u>are designing</u> <u>a large, new house</u>.

8. <u>A dark, mysterious stranger</u> entered <u>the room</u>.

9. He <u>shouldn't have gone dancing</u> <u>with her</u>.

10. <u>To make fun of others</u> is <u>his sport</u>.

(Answers on page 124)

Exercise 28—Phrases

Use the same instructions given for Exercise 1 on Phrases.

1. <u>The champion skier</u> <u>had drunk</u> <u>too much</u>.

2. <u>The fruit</u> rotted <u>within two days</u>.

3. He came <u>in a hurry</u> and sat <u>on his stool</u>.

4. <u>Her friends</u> <u>did come</u> <u>on time</u>.

5. She talks <u>as fast as possible</u>.

6. We spoke <u>about criminals</u> before we got <u>in the pool</u>.

7. We <u>hadn't heard</u> <u>about him</u> <u>since Wednesday</u>.

8. <u>The man</u> <u>with the oversized bat</u> <u>is leading</u> <u>in hits</u>.

9. We <u>haven't seen</u> him.

10. It was <u>a time of sorrow</u>.

(Answers on page 125)

The ABCs of English Grammar

Chapter 7

Functions of Speech

Functions to Review ————————————

The Subject

The subject of a sentence may be a word, a phrase, or a clause that names the person, place, thing, or idea, that the sentence is about. The subject will include a substantive. As mentioned previously (see page 32), the question to ask to find the subject of the sentence is either "**Who** are we talking about?" or "**What** are we talking about?"

Examples:

a. <u>Marcy</u> came home. ("Who?" Marcy)

b. <u>Travelling in Europe</u> was wonderful. ("What?" travelling in Europe)

c. <u>That she studied</u> was good. ("What?" That she studied)

d. The <u>book</u>, the <u>pencils</u>, the <u>ruler</u> and the <u>eraser</u> were there. (Here there are four nouns, making up a compound subject.)

The Predicate

The predicate of a sentence consists of a word, or group of words, that is essential to make an assertion about the subject (what the subject does, or what is being done to, or felt about, the subject).

Examples:

a. He <u>fainted</u>.

b. Christine <u>should</u> <u>be</u> <u>flying</u> a plane today.

c. He <u>seems</u> tired. (see page 78 for a discussion of subject complements after copula verbs.)

NOTE:
Remember that both subjects and predicates can be compound.

The ABCs of English Grammar

Example:

The <u>men</u> and <u>women</u> <u>sang</u> and <u>laughed</u>.

IMPORTANT REMINDER:
There must be at least one independent clause in order to have a sentence; sometimes, the subject may be understood.

Example:

"Take off!" (Here "you" is understood as the subject.)

IMPORTANT NOTE:
All of the above examples of subjects and predicates are of the simple subject (the basic word, or group of words, about which something is said), and the simple predicate (which consists only of the word, or group of words, essential to make an assertion about the subject). However, there may be a *complete subject*, which consists of the *simple subject* (a substantive), plus any modifiers (adjectives and adjective phrases) that are attached to it (to form a noun phrase), and a *complete predicate*, which is made up of the *simple predicate* (verb or verb phrase) plus all its modifiers (adverbs or adverb phrases) and/or complements.

Example:

<u>Sad and hungry, Tony</u> <u>sat down on the edge of the sidewalk.</u>

(The single underlining in the sentence is a complete subject, and "Tony" is the simple subject. The double underlining in the sentence is a complete predicate, and "sat" is the simple predicate.)

The Object of the Preposition

The preposition, as stated on page 14, connects a substantive (noun or pronoun) to some other element in the sentence. Every preposition, without exception, must have an object of the preposition which, also without exception, must be a substantive.

Examples:

a. He put the book (on) the shelf. (**Where** did he put the book? On the shelf. In this sentence **on** is the preposition connecting the verb *put* to the noun *shelf*, and *shelf* is the object of the preposition.)

b. The crown (of) his head is bald. (Here **of** is the preposition connecting the noun *crown* to the noun *head*, and *head* is the object of the preposition.)

c. Whom am I responsible (to)? (Here **to** is the preposition connecting the adjective *responsible* to the object pronoun *whom*, which is the object of the preposition.)

   Although the preposition is at the end of the sentence, there must still be an object of the preposition. Other constructions might make this particular object of the preposition more obvious.

   i   I am responsible (to) whom?

   ii (To) whom am I responsible?

d. He isn't the one I was looking for.
   (Here, the object of the preposition has to be understood; He isn't the one (for) whom I was looking.)

IMPORTANT NOTE:
All pronouns used as objects (direct and indirect objects will be detailed in the following two segments) must be in the objective case as follows:

me, you, her, him, us, them, whom

(See page 33 for a list of pronouns in the subjective case. For information on **who/whom**, see page 104.)

Other Functions of Speech

The Direct Object

The direct object is a word, or words (always including a substantive), that receive the action of the predicate's verb.

To find the direct object, ask "**Whom**?" (for people) or "**What**?" (for things) as indicated in the following examples.

Examples:

a. John hit the <u>ball</u>. ("John hit **whom**?" doesn't make sense. "John hit **what**?" immediately indicates "ball." Thus "ball" is the direct object.)

b. She saw <u>her</u>. ("She saw **whom**?" "Her" is the direct object.)

c. He kicked the <u>table</u> and <u>chair</u>. (Both "table" and "chair" answer the question, "He kicked **what**?" and, therefore, the direct object is compound.)

IMPORTANT NOTE:

1. All verbs that take objects are called <u>transitive</u> verbs. In the examples above, therefore, the verbs "to hit" and "to see" are transitive verbs as they have objects. Transitive verbs are indicated in the dictionary by "vt" or "v.t."

2. <u>Intransitive</u> verbs, which do not take objects, are indicated in the dictionary by "vi" or "v.i."

3. Some verbs can be both transitive and intransitive:

   a. She smells a rat. (vt)

   b. She smells good. (vi)

(In Example b, *good*, an adjective, functions as the subject complement. See page 78.)

The Indirect Object

The indirect object names the person or thing to whom, or on whose behalf, the action has been performed. The easiest way to find the indirect object is to ask "**To whom**" or "**To what?**" or "**For whom?**" or "**For what?**" of the verb.

Examples:

a. John gave <u>Ollie</u> the ball. ("John gave the ball **to what?**" doesn't work; "John gave the ball **to whom?**" does work because the answer is "Ollie," which is, therefore, the indirect object.)

b. She sent her <u>mother</u> and <u>father</u> the present. (She sent the present **to whom?**" The answer is "mother" and "father," so these two words form a compound indirect object.)

c. Mary lent <u>him</u> the book. ("Mary lent the book **to whom?**" The answer is "him," which is the indirect object.)

NOTE:
A reminder that, whether it's the object of the preposition, the direct object, or the indirect object, pronouns used as objects must be in the objective case. (See page 76.)

The Subject Complement

The subject complement is a noun, subject pronoun, or adjective that comes after a special verb called a **copula** (linking) verb, which completes the meaning of the verb. Here are the most common copula verbs:

to seem	to taste
to feel	to become
to appear	to look
to smell	to sound
to be	

Because the verb "to be" gives the greatest difficulty, I'm conjugating it (giving some of its different forms) as follows:

Person	Past Tense	Present Tense	Future Tense
I	was	am	will be
you	were	are	will be
he/she/it	was	is	will be
we	were	are	will be
they	were	are	will be

While "shall" might indicate more determination or emphasis in the future tense (*I shall win*), "will" is acceptable.

Examples:

a. She <u>seems</u> nice. (Here the adjective "nice" is the subject complement after the copula verb "seem.")

b. Marion <u>is</u> a boy. (Here the noun "boy" is the subject complement after the copula verb "is.")

c. It <u>was</u> they who left. (Here the pronoun "they" is the subject complement after the copula verb "was.")

NOTE:

1. A subject complement may be compound (have more than one word) such as in this sentence which has two adjectives: "It smells (good) and (clean)."

2. If the subject complement is a noun or pronoun, it is sometimes called the *predicate nominative*; if the subject complement is an adjective, it is sometimes called the *predicate adjective*.

3. If the main verb in a verb phrase is a copula verb, and a noun, pronoun, or adjective, follows it, the noun, pronoun, or adjective will be the subject complement.

Examples of #3

a. He <u>has</u> <u>become</u> a man. ("become" is not only the main verb, it is also a copula verb with the noun "man" as its subject complement.)

b. It <u>was</u> she. ("was" is the copula verb with the pronoun "she"—subjective case, see page 33—as its subject complement)

c. The picture <u>looks</u> good on the main shelf. ("looks" is a copula verb with the adjective "good" as its subject complement)

Exercise 29—Functions of Speech

On separate paper, have columns listed as follows: Subject, Predicate, Subject Complement, Direct Object, Indirect Object, and Object of the Preposition. Number each sentence and list the functions you find in the correct column.

1. The little boy asked for a Tickle Me Elmo.

2. It appeared good to me.

3. Mike offered Andy the pills.

4. He wouldn't take them. (Remember, "not" and its contraction "n't" are always adverbs.)

5. Mike offered Andy the pills, but he wouldn't take them. (Note there are two clauses here.)

6. Charlie ate the cookie on the table before his mother appeared.

7. When Sarah gave him the expensive gift, he was embarrassed about it.

8. The pimply man went down on one knee, and begged the sorceress for the magic cream.

9. He put the mixture in the pot on the stove, and it looked poisonous.

10. They will be tired when they arrive, so they'll want a rest.

(Answers on page 126)

Exercise 30—Functions of Speech

Follow the instructions given for Exercise 1 on Functions of Speech.

1. The boy rode his horse into the meadow where the animal could enjoy itself.

2. He didn't know the ones he wanted.

3. "It shall be done," the tired minister declared sadly, "but I can't guarantee when it will happen."

4. Although the group hadn't expected it, they accepted a ride on the truck from Harbinder.

5. "Mr. Smith will come in the morning, in the afternoon, whenever you want him," Mr. Brown told her.

6. "I have become sick of the same food," Rusty stated, "and I want a change, do you hear me?"

7. They had medicated the people on Tuesday, and had no wish for another visit. (Notice that the subject in the second clause is implied, not written, and is what is called an *elliptical*, or *understood*, subject).

8. The family burned the clothing in the fire because it was too filthy for use.

9. All looked for the dog, but their efforts were useless.

10. Gail has lent Gary the money, but I don't think he will pay her back.

(Answers on page 127)

NOTE:

"Loan" and "lent" are often confused. "Loan" is a noun; "lent" is the simple past tense of the verb "to lend."

Chapter 8

Extra Practice Exercises

Exercise 31—Parts of Speech

1. Rewrite each sentence.
2. Underline all nouns once.
3. Underline all verbs twice.
4. Draw parentheses around adjectives.
5. Draw brackets around adverbs.
6. Draw circles around pronouns.
7. Draw a "C" above conjunctions.
8. Draw a "P" above prepositions.
9. Draw an "A" above articles.
10. Draw an "I" above interjections.

1. "Yeah!" the young man yelled when he felt the power of the waves beneath him.

2. He didn't come, but I wasn't surprised.

3. The golden ruler belonged only to the king.

4. The family will give her everything before the year is finished.

5. Speedily, accurately, the determined mouse eagerly grabbed the mouldy cheese.

6. He sang because he wanted the money so he could go on vacation.

7. They must have gone into town, for none of us has seen them.

8. The angry grandmother yelled, "Get out of my pantry, you little brat!"

9. Susan went beyond the ordinary because she wanted success for Ron.

10. "Doesn't he need the money?" asked the disbelieving father.

(Answers on page 128)

Exercise 32—Sentence Structure

Rewrite each of the following sentences. Underline the subjects once, the predicates twice, and write after each sentence whether it is simple, compound, complex, or compound-complex.

1. "Michelle" is a popular name.

2. Jake and Bud ran and played in the park.

3. He went because his mother said she'd smack his face if he didn't.

4. Since he had pleaded, she joined him, but she brought her friend, too.

5. Although I like swordfish, there are other fish I prefer.

6. Whenever he giggled, he reminded me of a hyena, but I never told him.

7. The Deans travelled by car, but the Smiths travelled by bus.

8. See Pat, if you can, but don't tell her I gave you her address.

9. The young woman has little chance of making the most of herself, for she never went to school.

10. I can't come unless I get permission.

(Answers on page 129)

Exercise 33—Punctuation

Rewrite each of the following sentences with the required punctuation. (You might want to review Chapter 5 first.) Do not change the word order—or the capital letter on "Humor" in Sentence #11).

1. I sang I danced I acted I was the star of the evening

2. He showed us the following materials orlon rayon nylon cotton silk

3. It was a tiresome parade of fashions and I was sorry I attended the showing

4. Get out of here the naked man screamed Do you think you can just barge into my house without knocking

5. Chuck Johnson the ambulance attendant picked up the victim of an overdose at 520 am Sunday

6. The old man who used to love chess turned eighty-seven last week and he celebrated with a toast to himself

7. Mr McKay said his address was 3456 Welling St Auckland New Zealand

8. James looked at the crowd and smiled you'll never know what a great time I had here tonight he said

9. I've got to go but I don't have any idea of how to get to the bathroom sobbed the little girl

10. She bought a leather jacket boys shoes and mens pants

11. Mel Brooks was the person who said Humor is just another defence against the universe Martha Patterson said.

12. Its true the robin is in its nest she said but I don't have the courage to remove the body

13. One of the most famous television shows was All in the Family

14. He read the poem The Rape of the Lock and didnt understand a word

15. The London Times is a famous newspaper but I prefer others

(Answers on page 130)

Chapter 9

The Ten Most Common Errors in the English Language

Anyone who can conquer these errors should be able to offer a successful personal presentation to anyone else, whether in person or on paper.

The First Five Errors

The Incomplete Sentence

An incomplete sentence is one that does not have at least one independent clause. The subject might be missing, or the predicate, or both.

Examples:

a. With a special present. (This is an incomplete sentence because there is neither a subject nor a predicate. "<u>He</u> <u>came</u> with a special present" is an independent clause because a subject and a predicate have been added.)

b. <u>Was</u> <u>running</u> like a fearsome fiend. (This is an incomplete sentence because there is no subject. "<u>She</u> <u>was</u> <u>running</u> like a fearsome fiend" is an independent clause because there is a subject, a predicate, and the clause doesn't begin with a subordinating conjunction.)

IMPORTANT NOTE:
Remember that *and*, *but*, *for*, *or*, *nor*, *yet*, *so* are the coordinating conjunctions (see page 13), while the rest of the conjunctions are subordinating (for example, *while*, *although*, *until*, *after*).

Faulty Parallelism

Faulty parallelism is when dissimilar constructions are used to express similar ideas. Structure is parallel when a word, or clause, is balanced by at least one other of its own type.

Examples:

a. I will get there by car, bus or fly. (There are two nouns and then a verb; the construction would not contain faulty parallelism if similar constructions were used—in this case, all nouns. "I will get there by car, bus, or plane.")

b. He likes running and to swim. (Here the present participle of the verb "run" is followed by the infinitive form of the verb "swim," which is "to swim," and this causes the faulty parallelism. The correction could be "He likes running and swimming," or "He likes to run and to swim," or "He likes to run and swim.")

c. Sam was a caring teacher, a good teacher, and worked hard. (Here there are two adjectives, each followed by a noun, and then the sentence ends with a verb followed by an adverb. A correction would be, "Sam was a caring teacher, a good teacher, a hard worker.")

Faulty Subject-Verb Agreement

A verb must agree with its subject in number and person. Before further consideration of this type of error, note the following conjugation of "to be."

	Singular	Plural
First Person	I am	we are
Second Person	you are	you are
Third Person	he/she/it is	they are

When the subject of a sentence has, for example, a singular subject and a plural verb, there is a faulty subject-verb agreement.

Examples of Faulty Subject-Verb Agreement:

a. They is coming. (A plural subject requires a plural verb. The sentence should read, "They are coming." Alternatively, if the subject is singular, the verb should be singular: "He is coming.")

b. <u>Pork</u> and <u>beans</u> <u>are</u> his favorite food. (The two words, "pork" and "beans" function as a single unit and therefore require a singular verb: "<u>Pork</u> and <u>beans</u> <u>is</u> his favorite food.")

c. Either the <u>boy</u> or <u>I</u> <u>is</u> <u>planning</u> the party. (A compound subject joined by "or" or "nor" requires that the verb [simple predicate] agrees with the subject closer to it. The sentence should read, "Either the <u>boy</u> or <u>I</u> <u>am</u> <u>planning</u> the party.")

d. <u>Marian</u>, along with her seven sisters, six brothers, and fourteen cousins, <u>are</u> <u>coming</u> to visit. (If there are phrases or clauses set off with commas such as in this example, they must not change the required agreement of the subject and verb. The sentence should read, "<u>Marian</u>, along with her seven sisters, six brothers, and fourteen cousins, <u>is</u> <u>coming</u> for dinner.")

e. The <u>family</u> <u>are</u> <u>going</u>. (Nouns such as "family," "audience," and "class" take singular verbs if they are regarded as a unified group. The sentence should read, "The <u>family</u> <u>is</u> <u>going</u>.")

IMPORTANT NOTE:
Related to subject-verb agreement is the possessive adjective which must agree with the antecedent that controls its number.

Examples:

a. <u>Students</u> <u>must</u> <u>return</u> (their) books. (Here, the antecedent, or word that precedes the possessive adjective "their," is "students," which is plural.)

b. <u>Everyone</u> <u>must</u> <u>return</u> (her) book. (Here, the antecedent that precedes the possessive adjective "her" is "everyone," which is singular.)

c. Neither the <u>man</u> nor his <u>wife</u> <u>is</u> loving. (When a compound subject is joined by "or" or "nor" and "either" or "neither" precedes it, the verb should be singular.)

Comma Fault

A comma fault, also called a run-on sentence, or comma splice, occurs when two independent clauses have only a comma between them.

Example:

<u>I</u> <u>can't</u> <u>go</u> <u>skating</u>, my <u>skates</u> <u>are</u> dull.

The two independent clauses, having only a comma between them, are not connected properly. A correction could be made in any one of the following ways:

a. Put a semicolon instead of a comma between the clauses. (<u>I</u> <u>can't</u> <u>go</u> <u>skating</u> tonight; my <u>skates</u> <u>are</u> dull.)

b. Put a suitable coordinating conjunction after the comma which will connect the two clauses. (<u>I</u> <u>can't</u> <u>go</u> <u>skating</u> tonight, for my <u>skates</u> <u>are</u> dull.)

c. Make one of the clauses dependent by starting it with a subordinating conjunction. (<u>I</u> <u>can't</u> <u>go</u> <u>skating</u> tonight because my <u>skates</u> <u>are</u> dull.)

d. If the two clauses are not similar in subject, the best way to correct a comma fault is to have two, separate sentences. (<u>I</u> <u>can't</u> <u>go</u> <u>skating</u> tonight. <u>Did</u> <u>you</u> <u>know</u> <u>Fred</u> <u>is</u> sick?)

Ellipsis

Ellipsis as used here (and allied to the definition in Chapter 5) is when a word, or words, necessary to complete the meaning of the sentence is left out. (See page 64.)

Examples:

a. Joan's car was stolen while travelling in Oregon. (Cars can't operate independently. A suitable correction would be, "Joan's car was stolen while <u>she</u> was travelling in Oregon.")

b. André is nicer than any of his family. (André is a <u>member</u> of the family, so he can't be nicer than himself. A suitable correction would be, "André is nicer than any <u>other</u> member of his family.")

Exercise 34—The First Five Errors

Rewrite each of the sentences correctly; then, in parentheses at the end of each sentence, state the type of error that you found in the original sentence.

1. Molly and she is going to have a good evening.

2. He had a great time, I hope she did.

3. They like kissing and to hug.

4. With laughing eyes.

5. The razor was lost when in the store.

6. Kwame, plus all his family and friends, are going skiing this week-end.

7. Jasper was a good tarantula, a safe tarantula, and was healthy.

8. Her marks are improving, she must be learning something.

9. Down by the birth control clinic.

10. After hiking in California.

(Answers on page 131)

Exercise 35—The First Five Errors

Follow the same instructions given for Exercise 1.

1. Should have been seen going running from the freaks.

2. Both boys like cruising and to party.

3. He goes to rock concerts, I don't.

4. My list of reasons are long.

5. John eats organ meat, I can't stand watching him.

6. Queenie is bigger than any dog in the kennel.

7. In the midst of a tropical heat wave.

8. She loves to rap and wrestling.

9. Each must return his or her book, there will be a fine.

10. Neither the man nor his girlfriend are happy.

(Answers on page 132)

The Second Five Errors ———————

Dangling Modifiers

A dangling modifier is a group of words that does not refer to anything in the sentence, or refers to a word to which it is not logically related.

Examples:

a. After opening the oven door, the turkey cooked more slowly. ("After opening the oven door" is a dangling modifier because there is no suitable word for the phrase to modify as a turkey is unlikely to open an oven door.) To correct this error, a suitable subject is necessary: After I opened the oven door, the turkey cooked more slowly.

b. Walking down the street, the house was admired. ("Walking down the street" is a dangling modifier because houses can't walk down streets.) The way to correct the error is to include a suitable subject as follows:
Walking down the street, we admired the house.

Faulty Reference of Pronoun

A pronoun must agree with its antecedent in number (singular or plural), gender (male, female, neuter) and case (which means that pronouns used as direct objects, indirect objects, or objects of the preposition, should be in the objective case, while pronouns used as subjects and subject complements should be put in the subjective case). If it doesn't, there is a faulty reference of pronoun. (See pages 33 and 76.)

Examples:

a. John told his father he would soon be feeling better. (Here we don't know whether the pronoun *he* refers to *John* or *father*. An easy way to correct this faulty reference of pronoun is to use quotation marks as follows: John said, "Dad, I will soon be feeling better."
or
"Dad, you will soon be feeling better.")

b. If your parents don't like our activities, they should be stopped. (What is going to be stopped? The parents? The activities? Due to the fact that we don't know whether *they* refers to *parents* or *activities*, this sentence contains a faulty reference of pronoun. A correction could be: "We should stop our activities if your parents dislike them.")

Illiteracies

Illiteracies are words or phrases that have no real meaning in the spoken or written language.

Examples:

a. Irregardless, I am not happy. (As there is no word "irregardless" in the English language, this term is regarded as an illiteracy. The correction would be, "Regardless, I am not happy.")

b. I don't got none. (This is an illiteracy, often referred to as a double negative. The problem is that there are two negatives, "n't" and "none," in the clause. The correction would be: "I don't have any," or "I have none.")

c. "Have you seen what's-his-face?" (There is no real meaning here. "Have you seen the tall, dark man with the white, curly hair?" would be more acceptable.)

Tense Shifts

"Tense" always refers to verbs and indicates the time of action, whether past, present, or future. If the tenses are shifted from one to another without any logic in a sentence, the result can be confusing.

Examples:

a. We took our seats while the guide explains the designs of the temples. (The first verb, "took," is in the past tense, while the second verb, "explains," is in the present tense. A correction might be "We took our seats while the guide explained the designs of the temples.")

b. When the doors were closed, we are in total darkness. (The first verb is in the past tense, while the second is in the present tense. A correction might be, "The doors were closed, and we were in total darkness.")

Grammatical Errors That Destroy Meaning

"G. E. T. D. M." refers to errors in grammar that cause the clarity of the sentence to be confused or destroyed.

Examples:

a. The family gave we a warm reception. (Here the subject pronoun "we" is used as an indirect object, which confuses the meaning. The object pronoun "us" should have been used.)

b. Between you and I, the party was a blast. (Here the meaning is confused because "between" is a preposition which requires an object and, in this case, the object pronoun "me" must be used.)

Exercise 36—The Second Five Errors

Rewrite each of the following sentences correctly. At the end of each, in parentheses, state the type of error evident in the original sentence. (Although there may be more than one correct method for rewriting, there would be no variation in the type of error.)

1. After calling the airport, the flight was postponed.

2. I came after she calls me.

3. The children brought joy for you and I.

4. He said, "Anyways, that's my story."

5. Her sister told Mary she would soon have her baby.

6. To enjoy jogging, shoes must be of good quality.

7. The teacher advised the student that he would get AIDS unless he was more careful.

8. "Not never will we betray our country," the man said.

9. They smile when he belched.

10. He gave the present to they.

(Answers on page 132)

Exercise 37—The Second Five Errors

Follow the same instructions given for Exercise 1.

1. The hunter went into the woods and sees a deer.

2. On entering the room, a beautiful picture was seen.

3. John and him are going.

4. He said he didn't got none.

5. She wore a ribbon in her hair which was red.

6. When covered in syrup, you will enjoy the tasty dish.

7. Nate told his friend he should put some money into the machine.

8. Carving carefully, the turkey looked delicious.

9. The girl is terrified and began to resist.

10. My father scolded Harry and I.

(Answers on page 133)

Chapter 10

A Few Additions for Enrichment

Verbs—Active and Passive Voice

The "voice" of a verb indicates whether the subject of the verb acts or is acted upon. Basically, active voice indicates that the subject of the verb is the actor, or doer, while the passive voice indicates that the subject was acted upon, or was the receiver of the action.

	Active Voice	Passive Voice
Present Tense	I ask I am asking I do ask	I am asked I am being asked
Past Tense	I asked I was asking I did ask	I was asked I was being asked
Future Tense	I shall* ask I will* be asking	I shall* be asked I will* be asked
Present Perfect Tense	I have asked I have been asking	I have been asked
Past Perfect Tense	I had asked I had been asking	I had been asked
Future Perfect Tense	I will* have asked I shall* have been asking	I shall* have been asked I will* have been asked

* Either "shall" or "will" may be used.

Verbals

Definition

Verbals are words which are partly verb and partly another part of speech. They can be substantives (naming words) or modifiers (describing words).

Gerunds

The gerund, a substantive ending in *ing*, may be described as a verbal noun; namely, it is half verb and half noun. Like all verbals, it cannot function by itself as the predicate of a sentence. However, it can function as the subject, object of a verb, object of a preposition, or subject complement. The thing that a gerund names is action, or being, and thus it functions as a verb. The four examples below are in the present active case.

Examples:

a. Remembering is hard for Fred. (Here the gerund *remembering* functions as the subject.)

b. I heard the shooting. (Here the gerund *shooting* functions as the direct object.)

c. Were they jailed for stealing? (Here the gerund *stealing* functions as the object of the preposition *for*.)

d. Her love is singing. (Here the gerund *singing* functions as the subject complement.)

NOTE:

Here are the four forms of the gerund. Note that in the forms other than the present active, *ing* is attached to one of the other words in the combination:

Present Active: writing
Present Passive: being written
Perfect Active: having written
Perfect Passive: having been written

The ABCs of English Grammar

Participles

The participle (detailed on page 9) used as a modifier may be described as a verbal adjective: namely, it is half verb and half adjective. As participles modify substantives, they function like adjectives. The participle modifies by describing the substantive as performing or receiving action, or existing in a state of being; thus it functions like a verb.

Examples:

a. The rushing wind whipped the leaves off the trees. (Here the participle *rushing* modifies the noun *wind*.)

b. Jim, having been elected, was a happy man. (Here the participle *having been elected* modifies the noun *Jim*.)

An adverb may modify a participle.

Examples:

a. The wind, rushing wildly, whipped the leaves off the trees. (*wildly*, an adverb, modifies the participle *rushing*.)

b. Moving quietly, the army came closer to the enemy. (Here the adverb *quietly* modifies the participle *moving*.)

NOTE:
Here are five forms of the participle. In the passive forms, the words "being" and "having been" are often omitted.

Present Participle, Active: knowing
Present Participle, Passive: being known
Past Participle, Active: having known
Past Participle, Passive: known
Perfect Participle, Passive: having been known

Infinitives

The infinitive is a verbal which functions as a noun, an adjective, or an adverb. In every case, the infinitive shares the function of a verb by stating action or being. Note that the infinitive is preceded by "to" which is called the sign of the infinitive.

Examples:

a. *To travel* is fun. (Here the infinitive "to travel" is the subject.)

b. They do not want *to travel*. (Here the infinitive "to travel" functions as a direct object.)

c. We found the money *to go*. (Here the infinitive "to go" functions as an adjective modifying the noun "money.")

d. The whole family hated *to leave*. (Here the infinitive "to leave" functions as an adverb modifying the verb "hated.")

NOTE:
Do not confuse "to," which is a preposition, with "to," which is the sign of the infinitive.

Noun Clauses

A noun clause is a dependent clause that performs the function of a noun.

Examples:

a. That he would come was evident. ("That he would come" is a noun clause operating as the subject of the sentence.)

b. He feels he knows the truth. (Here "he knows the truth" is the subject complement of the copula verb "feels." While "he knows the truth" appears at first glance to be an independent clause, it is easy to see with a second glance that the relative pronoun "that" is understood before "he knows the truth."

c. He said that he would go. (In this example, "that he would go" is the direct object of the verb "said.")

Nonrestrictive Appositives —

Commas are used before and after nonrestrictive appositives. A nonrestrictive appositive gives additional information about the noun it follows, but is not necessary to identify that noun.

Examples:

a. My younger brother, a clever man, is now a hotel manager. (The nonrestrictive appositive, "a clever man," is not essential to the meaning.)

b. Ms. Marcy Robinson, the smartest girl in school, got married. (The nonrestrictive appositive, "the smartest girl in school," is not essential to the news that Marcy got married.)

Restrictive Appositives —

A restrictive appositive gives additional information about the substantive it follows and is necessary in order to identify that substantive; thus restrictive appositives are not set off with commas.

Examples:

a. He asked Ted my husband, not Ted my cousin. (Both "my husband" and "my cousin" are restrictive appositives, and both are needed to find out which Ted is which.)

b. The picture covered with dust is my favorite. (Because it allows identification of the particular picture and therefore is essential, "covered with dust" is a restrictive appositive.)

Who/Whom

Such clauses as "I want," "he thinks," and "they know" may follow either *who*, a subject pronoun, or *whom*, an object pronoun. The choice depends on the way *who* or *whom* is used in its own clause.

Examples:

a. Beth is a girl whom they know. (In the second clause, *whom* is the direct object of the verb *know*. This example may be compared with the clause construction "They know Beth." The object pronoun *whom* stands for the direct object, *Beth*.)

b. Beth is a girl who we think is nice. (Here in the second clause, *who* is the subject of the verb *is*. This is more evident when the three clauses, one of them split, are listed: 1) Beth is a girl; 2) we think; 3) who is nice. The subject pronoun *who* stands for the subject, *Beth*.)

The ABCs of English Grammar

Answers to Exercises

Exercise 1—Nouns

1. The <u>group</u> swam in <u>Lake Okanagan</u> on <u>Friday</u>.

2. The <u>boy</u> bought a <u>Speedo</u> and <u>goggles</u> at the <u>store</u>.

3. When I drove the <u>tractor</u> into the <u>barn</u>, I knew my <u>father</u> would be angry.

4. <u>Mr. Jackson</u> usually spent every <u>day</u> of the <u>summer</u> wrestling <u>alligators</u>.

5. My <u>family</u> saw <u>Grant Hill</u> play <u>basketball</u>.

6. <u>Uncle Duncan</u> came at <u>Christmas</u> and brought my <u>brother</u> a <u>lot</u> of <u>presents</u>.

7. When the <u>Nakanishis</u> visited <u>British Columbia</u>, they went to <u>Long Beach</u> and <u>Victoria</u>.

8. My <u>friends</u> picked <u>strawberries</u> last <u>summer</u> and said their <u>backs</u> ached from the <u>work</u>.

9. With a <u>sailboat</u>, <u>Jill</u> has no <u>need</u> of a <u>motor</u>.

10. When <u>Bobby</u> goes to the <u>fair</u>, he has a <u>ball</u>.

Exercise 2—Nouns

1. "<u>Ed</u>, would you like another <u>dish</u> of <u>yogurt</u>?"

2. In the <u>barn</u>, the <u>cat</u> had a <u>feast</u> of <u>rats</u>.

3. The <u>girl</u> loved making <u>models</u> of <u>biplanes</u> and <u>triplanes</u>.

4. <u>Andrea</u> loves <u>swimming</u> and <u>fishing</u>.

5. Her <u>parents</u> tried to prepare the <u>girl</u> for the worst <u>news</u> of her <u>life</u>.

6. There were <u>hundreds</u> of <u>people</u> held by <u>guerrillas</u> at the <u>Japanese Embassy</u> in <u>Lima</u>, <u>Peru</u>.

7. <u>Martin</u> and <u>Jack</u> went to <u>Whistler</u>, <u>British Columbia</u>, for a <u>vacation</u>.

8. "This <u>sentence</u> has a <u>total</u> of five <u>nouns</u>, according to my <u>count</u>," the <u>student</u> said.

The ABCs of English Grammar

9. The <u>group</u> was told that their first <u>dance</u> would take place the following <u>week</u>.

10. At the <u>restaurant</u>, the <u>students</u> proved that their <u>eyes</u> weren't bigger than their <u>stomachs</u>.

Exercise 3—Pronouns

1. I, what*, you, This, mine

2. They

3. we, them, we, this, that

4. she

5. Those, yours, this, mine

6. It

7. She, everyone, some, you,

8. they, her, she

9. Each, us, he, them

10. We, whatever*, we, these, ours

    * These are difficult; check dictionary for pronoun meanings.

Exercise 4—Pronouns

1. This, I, any, you

2. They, something

3. Some, them, none

4. This, ours, he

5. He, many, them

6. We, those, they, we, these

7. Which, you, me

8. It, mine, I, it

9. All, us

10. Everybody, who, it

Exercise 5—Verbs

1. Fumiko <u>smiled</u> when she <u>saw</u> the size of it.

2. Franz <u>had</u> <u>cooked</u> the cat when he <u>was</u> <u>starving</u>.

3. She <u>has</u> <u>skated</u> for three hours.

4. She <u>has</u> <u>burned</u> her left buttock.

5. The family <u>had</u> <u>gone</u> to a counsellor.

6. The family <u>should</u> <u>have</u> <u>gone</u> to a psychiatrist.

7. We <u>could</u> <u>have</u> <u>spotted</u> the mouse if we <u>had</u> <u>looked</u>.

8. I <u>shall</u> <u>ask</u> him for money.

9. Everybody at the picnic <u>had</u> <u>eaten</u>.

10. We <u>will</u> <u>see</u> him next week.

Exercise 6—Verbs

<u>Auxiliary Verbs</u>	<u>Main Verbs</u>
1. has	lit
2. have been	asking
3. shall have	danced
4. could have had	played been
5. may have was	guessed
6. had had	waved blown
7. do had	want stated

The ABCs of English Grammar

8. Do   want
  asked

9. have   fished
  have   caught

10. had been   found

Exercise 7—Verbs

Present Tense	Past Tense	Past Participle	Present Participle
1. laugh	laughed	laughed	laughing
2. freeze	froze	frozen	freezing
3. fall	fell	fallen	falling
4. drink	drank	drunk	drinking
5. bring	brought	brought	bringing
6. break	broke	broken	breaking
7. shrink	shrank	shrunk	shrinking
8. lead	led	led	leading
9. swim	swam	swum	swimming
10. write	wrote	written	writing

Exercise 8—Prepositions

1. It was hard for us.

2. He stood in front of the door and wouldn't let us enter the house.

3. We work during rain, hail, sleet or snow.

4. Sukhpal lived on a farm when he was little.

5. She spoke to them.

6. He dropped his cigarette, then ran towards the bus stop. (or, if you considered "bus" an adjective, just "stop")

7. She announced the news (of) the |party|, but nobody was interested.

8. The cup fell (from) the |counter| and broke.

9. He spoke (concerning) the |question| but nobody understood him.

10. "I'll stay (for) a |while|," said her friend, hugging her.

Exercise 9—Prepositions

1. Janet <u>went</u> (to) the |game|.

2. The horse <u>galloped</u> (across) the |beach|.

3. We loved the <u>grin</u> (on) his |face|.

4. The car <u>seems</u> (in) fine |condition|.

5. My father <u>punished</u> Jim (for) his |mistake|.

6. He <u>stood</u> (above) |Tom|.

7. Shane repaired the <u>roof</u> (of) the |house|.

8. We saw the <u>dog</u> (from) the |pound|.

9. Jane was <u>kind</u> (to) |Rochester|.

10. The falcon <u>swooped</u> (between) the |trees|.

Exercise 10—Prepositions

1. She <u>went</u> (down) the |road| and (into) the |restaurant|.

2. David <u>threw</u> the ball (on) the |floor|, and then he <u>stepped</u> (on) his |cue| and broke it.

3. <u>Mr. Joe</u> was (beside) the |store| when he saw an <u>accident</u> (down) the |street|.

4. You deserve the blue <u>ribbon</u> (for) that |animal|.

5. (For) that |animal|, you deserve the blue <u>ribbon</u>.

6. He <u>jumped</u> (from) the garage |roof| and <u>landed</u> (on) a sharp |twig|.

7. He is a <u>violinist</u> (beyond) |expectation|, and I have great <u>hopes</u> (for) |him|.

8. The <u>man</u> (behind) <u>him</u> <u>saw</u> the problem (before) the <u>others</u>.

9. (In) the <u>ditch</u>, <u>covered</u> (with) <u>mud</u>, the dwarf <u>lay</u> still.

10. He <u>came</u> (through) the <u>operation</u> and <u>recovered</u> (within) two <u>weeks</u>.

Exercise 11—Review on Nouns, Pronouns, Verbs, Conjunctions and Prepositions

	Nouns	Pron's	Verbs	Conj's	Prep's
1.	Jane	she	ordered		with
	salmon		asked	and	for
	vegetables				
	dessert				
2.	boat	they	loved	because	
	chance	it	gave		at
	freedom	them			
3.	Frank	you	will		
	pill		give		in
	morning		said		
	man				
4.	Rani	you	will	when	
		she	call		
		them	needs		
5.	meeting	he	has		
		he	been	while	
			shall		
			attend		
6.	men	they	will	and	
	women		come	whenever	
	children	everyone	can	because	
	excitement		loves		

	Nouns	Pron's	Verbs	Conj's	Prep's
7.	relatives	we	should	and	on
	Monday		arrive		
	dinner	they	hope		before
			can		
			come		
8.	city	nobody	had	although	
	snow	it	expected		
			was		
			covered		in
9.	weekend	I	will	but	by
			go		
		I	must		
			return		
10.	men	she	left	before	
	Stephanie	they	awoke	and	
	trouble		knew		
			were		
			heading		for

Exercise 12—Review on Nouns, Pronouns, Verbs, Conjunctions and Prepositions

	Nouns	Pron's	Verbs	Conj's	Prep's
1.	mood	it	felt	whenever	in
	eagle		would		above
	peak		fly		
2.	tools	I	put	until	beneath
	bench	them	have		for
	space				in
	cupboard				
3.	Greg	each	studied	and	into
	Brett	them	was	because	of
	night		terrified		of
	failure				

The ABCs of English Grammar

	Nouns	Pron's	Verbs	Conj's	Prep's
4.	snow Jean-Paul	we	searched could find	but	under
5.	tree arbutus berries leaves bark	I it	know is sheds	because and	
6.	year hill exercise houses lake	we	climb stare	and	during for at beyond
7.	traffic	all they	will come are caught	unless	in
8.		you you it	eat go can manage	before if	
9.	Laurie Nordstrom telephone	you she she you	were gone came said would call	while but	on
10.	game Jim Buck problem	we	will play causes	when or	

Exercise 13—Adjectives

1. magnificent

2. small, twisted

3. wicked, pleasant

4. shimmering, gleaming

5. athletic, ancient

6. long, rambling, meaningless

7. spotted, green

8. beloved, long ("detox" acceptable, as it could be regarded as an adjective, and not a noun)

9. Tired, desperate

10. Those, beautiful

Exercise 14—Adjectives

1. different

2. tall, blue-eyed

3. this

4. graceful

5. these

6. rewarding, many, grinning

7. large, small, greedy, old

8. ten, twelve

9. second, long-distance

10. each, expensive

Exercise 15—Adverbs

1. loudly

2. later

3. hard, well

4. extremely

5. very, cautiously

6. wildly, lovingly

7. most, kindly

8. once, never, again

9. marvellously, happily

10. apprehensively

Exercise 16—Adverbs

1. modestly

2. shrilly, viciously

3. particularly, fast

4. cleanly

5. rather, terminally

6. extremely, uncontrollably, dearly

7. more, speedily

8. exceptionally

9. somewhat, better

10. seriously, immediately

Exercise 17—Using All Parts of Speech

1. "Aha!" exclaimed a (smiling) Sherlock Holmes. "I think [now] I understand!"

2. [Quietly], the (small) girl entered the (dusty) room and put the (plastic) statue on the table.

3. He has[n't] given me a thing; [however], as I expected nothing, I was without disappointment.

4. Please tell them if anybody should come.

5. The boys came [later], and we were (glad) when they arrived.

6. He [carefully] placed the (heavy) book [back] in the (lower) drawer, [then] turned [around].

7. All felt [gloriously] (happy) whenever they rode (their) bicycles.

8. Mrs. Conway [neatly] removed the leg of the turkey with the (sharpened) knife.

9. "I'm [always] (happy) when we're finished with winter and begin the glory of spring."

10. "This is a treat, Mrs. Moon," the (smiling) boy said as he [happily] raised (his) fork. "I [never] expected pie!"

Exercise 18—Using All Parts of Speech

1. (He) <u>was</u> a (delightful) <u>baby</u> and [rarely] <u>cried</u> at <u>night</u>.
   - A: was, C: baby, P: night

2. (Who) <u>pushed</u> the (colored) <u>pencil</u> into the (cracked) <u>wood</u> of the (ancient) <u>desk</u>?
   - A: pushed, P: pencil, A: wood, P: desk, A: desk

3. "Oh!" the (startled) <u>girl</u> <u>exclaimed</u>. (I) <u>am</u> [absolutely] <u>terrified</u> of <u>snakes</u>!"
   - I: Oh, A: girl, A: am, P: snakes

4. (Whoever) the <u>woman</u> <u>was</u>, (she) <u>knew</u> with <u>certainty</u> that the (large) <u>family</u> <u>was</u> in (serious) <u>difficulty</u>.
   - A: woman, P: knew, C: certainty, A: certainty, P: family, P: difficulty

5. "<u>Is</u> (somebody) <u>coming</u> on <u>Thursday</u>, <u>Mom</u>?" the (little) <u>girl</u> <u>asked</u> [eagerly].
   - P: coming, A: asked

6. (We) <u>wandered</u> [aimlessly] and <u>did</u>[n't] <u>worry</u> about (it).
   - C: wandered, P: worry

7. (They) <u>sat</u> [down] in the <u>hope</u> (their) <u>lawyer</u> <u>would</u> <u>listen</u> to (their) (unbelievable) <u>story</u>.
   - P: hope, A: lawyer, P: story

8. (Each) <u>leaned</u> [quietly] against the <u>tree</u> before (he) <u>made</u> (his)(final) <u>decision</u>.
   - P: tree, A: tree, C: made

9. "The <u>parcel</u> <u>should</u> <u>have</u> <u>arrived</u> (last) <u>Thursday</u>, <u>should</u>[n't] (it)?"
   - A: parcel

10. The (loving) <u>father</u> <u>glowed</u> [happily] as (his) (young) <u>daughter</u> <u>went</u> to the <u>stage</u> for (her) (bronze) <u>medallion</u>.
    - A: father, C: daughter, P: went, A: stage, P: medallion

Exercise 19—Clauses

1. (He __wrote__ a novel), and (it __was__ wild.)
   - IC / IC

2. (The __parcel came__)(when I __was__ away.)
   - IC / DC

3. (While __she waited__), (she __set__ the VCR.)
   - DC / IC

4. (I __hate__ it)(whenever __you spit__ on me.)
   - IC / DC

5. (We __know__ the artist); (his __name is__ Georges Costaz.)
   - IC / IC

6. (Before __she put__ the tent up), (the __storm began.__)
   - DC / IC

7. (The __men recognized__ the thief)(who __had stolen__ their money.)
   - IC / DC

8. (Mr. __Jackson participated__), (although __he has regretted__ it since.)
   - IC / DC

9. (Whenever __he can__), (Joe __swings__ with the crowd.)
   - DC / IC

10. (Because __you said__ it), (I __will believe__ it.)
    - DC / IC

Exercise 20—Clauses

1. (Won-bin and Chi-woong __go__) (whenever __they can.__)
   - IC / DC

2. (The whole __family studies__ clams and oysters.)
   - IC

3. (Before __Elizabeth arrived__), (Mother and Dad __had prepared__ her room.)
   - DC / IC

4. (The <u>man</u> and his <u>wife</u> **IC** <u>have</u> <u>sold</u> their house.)

5. (When our <u>friends</u> **DC** <u>visited</u>), (<u>we</u> **IC** <u>played</u> bridge.)

6. (Both <u>boys</u> and <u>girls</u> **IC** <u>cooked</u> and <u>cleaned</u>.)

7. (<u>He</u> **IC** <u>was</u> unhappy) (after <u>you</u> **DC** <u>jumped</u> insanely on his car hood last week.)

8. (Unless <u>he</u> **DC** <u>has</u> an accident), (<u>Harry</u> **IC** <u>will</u> <u>be</u> <u>going</u>.)

9. (While <u>he</u> **DC** <u>was</u> <u>thinking</u> about the problem), (<u>he</u> <u>was</u> <u>distracted</u> **IC** by a sting on his neck.)

10. (Since <u>you</u> and <u>Rita</u> <u>went</u> to Toronto), (<u>Jane</u> and <u>I</u> **IC** <u>have</u> <u>missed</u> you.)

Exercise 21—Clauses

1. (While <u>they</u> **DC** <u>were</u> there), (<u>they</u> **IC** <u>enjoyed</u> the people), and (<u>they</u> **IC** <u>loved</u> the climate.)

2. (<u>Mr.</u> <u>Pai</u> **IC** <u>asked</u> the man)(when the <u>train</u> **DC** <u>arrived</u>), but (<u>he</u> **IC** <u>received</u> no definite answer.)

3. (Our <u>groups</u> **IC** <u>stayed</u> together), and (<u>we</u> all **IC** <u>went</u> to the beach) (whenever <u>we</u> **DC** <u>could</u>.)

4. (<u>Have</u> <u>you</u> **IC** <u>seen</u> her), or (<u>have</u> <u>you</u> **IC** <u>seen</u> Bix) (since <u>we</u> last **DC** <u>met</u>)?

5.   **DC**   **IC**

5. (Because I am familiar with him), (I recommend him), and

    IC   **DC***

(I think)(you will like him.)

6.   **IC**   **IC**   **IC**

6. (She does know Simmer), (I know Susan), and (we both know Shing.)

7.   **DC**   **IC**

7. (Whenever Sam gets a job), (he keeps it only two or three days)

    DC

(before he loses it.)

8.   **IC**   **DC**

8. (They will look for the treasure)(after they have located the map)

    DC*

(they received in the mail.)

9.   **IC**   **DC**   **IC**

9. (I remember)(when I last saw her), for (it was my birthday.)

10.   **DC**   **IC**

10. (Whenever he yells), (the children and dogs run) (until they can

    DC

hear him no longer.)

* A reminder that the relative pronoun leading these clauses is understood.

Exercise 22—The Four Basic Types of Sentences

    IC   **DC**

1. (We met)(whenever we could.)—Complex

             IC

2. (Céline Dion delivered a fantastic performance.)—Simple

    DC   **IC**

3. (Wherever he goes), (my thoughts will not be with him.)

—Complex

4. (We should have gone on the cruise), and (I wish)(we had.)
   IC ... **IC** **DC**
   —Compound-Complex

5. (When we saw the delightful puppy), (we couldn't resist her.)
   DC ... **IC**
   —Complex

6. "Give me my money now!")—Simple (subject is "you" understood)
   IC

7. (He will come), or (I will drag him here.)—Compound
   IC ... **IC**

8. (Bert said)(the man was handsome and smart), but (I could
   IC **DC** ... **IC**
   never love a wimp.)—Compound-Complex

   ("that" understood before "the man")

9. (Although I loved the motorcycle), (I sold it) (because I feared)
   DC ... **IC** ... **DC**
   (I would have another accident.)—Complex
   DC

10. (Until he saw the photograph of himself), (he hadn't realized)
    DC ... **IC**
    (that he had bowed legs) — Complex
    DC

Exercise 23—Sentence Tones

1. imperative/period or exclamatory/exclamation mark

2. declarative/period

3. interrogative/question mark

4. exclamatory/exclamation mark or declarative/period

5. interrogative/question mark (While you might want to put an exclamation mark here, the question mark must be added to the sentence because there is a question involved. Never write both an exclamation mark and a question mark after a sentence.)

6. declarative/period

7. exclamatory/exclamation mark

8. declarative/period (If the situation is a county fair or something similar; if offered in response to an exaggerating speaker, an exclamation mark, making an exclamatory sentence is in order.)

9. declarative/period

10. imperative/period (If the speaker is excited, an exclamation mark might be in order.)

Exercise 24—Punctuation

1. "Go away, Harry," the boy said.

2. "Susan, do you believe I'm a mentally challenged person?" her mother asked.

3. Whenever Mr. Fraley eats figs, he gets diarrhea.

4. He can go, but you can't.

5. "Let me think—no, I don't think I can think," Mrs. Jones admitted. (or, "Let me think, no, I don't think I can think," Mrs. Jones admitted.)

6. Everyone was shocked when the woman said, "Thousands of animals a month are killed for medical research."

7. Beyond the fence, past the bridge, through the meadow, I continued to walk towards town.

8. Nancy Taylor, who was once a dancer, earned a medical degree.

9. The dog was short, fat, adorable and incontinent.

10. Adrian Felton lives at 2605 West King Edward Street, in Vancouver, British Columbia.

Exercise 25—Punctuation

1. "You think I wouldn't do that?" she asked as she laughed in his miserable face.

2. In January 1972, East Pakistan became the Republic of Bangladesh.

3. "Are you saying you have cheated?" the teacher asked. "Go to the principal's office now!"

4. "He has gone back to the mountains," the man said, "and I am going back, too."

5. Maurice Greene, from Granada Hills, California, ran the 100 meter race in a record 9.79 seconds.

6. Huge, black, frothing, the enraged bull managed to gore my right thigh with his left horn.

7. Mr. Yates, if you want my opinion, is a loud-mouthed pain in the butt.

8. She went, so I went, but I was sorry, and so was she.

9. She wrote Barbara G. Smith, M.D., at the bottom of the prescription.

10. Travelling at 80 mph, (m.p.h. is another, acceptable choice) he finally stopped to set his watch to Mountain Standard Time.

Exercise 26—Punctuation

1. This is a good idea, and Antonio agrees. (It doesn't matter if you have this in quotation marks.)

2. John F. Kennedy was assassinated on November 22, 1963.

3. He travelled 80 kph through the slums of Halifax, Nova Scotia.

4. "Well, Pierre," the man said, "I think we should leave no later than 6:40 p.m."

5. "Go back to your own house!" the man yelled at the dog. "Do I have to kick you?"

6. "Get out of my sight, you pathetic piece of trash!" the secretary told the computer expert.

7. *Star Wars* was a movie released exactly forty years after *Snow White and the Seven Dwarfs*.

8. If you decide to stay at this camp, there are four rules: don't leave the camp without permission; always travel with a buddy; be on time for meals; clean up your cabin. (commas could replace the semi-colons, except for the last one which could be replaced by a comma plus the coordinating conjunction, "and.")

9. I love peaches, pears and apples.

10. "Did Molly say, 'Please come on Thursday'?" Julia asked. "I just can't remember."

Exercise 27—Phrases

1. in the morning—adverb phrase

2. the boy—noun phrase
   had seen—verb phrase

3. raising her fist—adjective phrase
   the angry girl—noun phrase
   towards the boy—adverb phrase

4. a delicious Granny Smith apple—noun phrase

5. that book—noun phrase
   on the desk—adjective phrase

6. the buffalo—noun phrase
   through the mud—adverb phrase

7. are designing—verb phrase
   a large, new house—noun phrase

8. a dark, mysterious stranger—noun phrase
   the room—noun phrase

9. shouldn't have gone dancing—verb phrase
   with her—adverb phrase

10. to make fun of others—noun phrase
    his sport—noun phrase

Exercise 28—Phrases

1. the champion skier—noun phrase
   had drunk—verb phrase
   too much—adverb phrase

2. the fruit—noun phrase
   within two days—adverb phrase

3. in a hurry—adverb phrase
   on his stool—adverb phrase

4. Her friends—noun phrase
   did come—verb phrase
   on time—adverb phrase

5. as fast as possible—adverb phrase

6. about criminals—adverb phrase
   in the pool—adverb phrase

7. hadn't heard—verb phrase
   about him—adverb phrase
   since Wednesday—adverb phrase

8. the man—noun phrase
   with the oversized bat—adjective phrase
   is leading—verb phrase
   in hits—adverb phrase

9. haven't seen—verb phrase

10. a time of sorrow—noun phrase*

    *See Subject Complement on pages 78 and 79.

Exercise 29—Functions of Speech

Subject	Predicate	Subject Complement	Direct Object	Indirect Object	Object of Prep.
1. boy	asked				Tickle Me Elmo
2. It	appeared	good			me
3. Mike	offered		pills	Andy	
4. He	would take		them		
5. Mike	offered		pills	Andy	
he	would take		them		
6. Charlie	ate		cookie		table
mother	appeared				
7. Sarah	gave		gift	him	
he	was embarrassed				it
8. man	went				knee
	begged		sorceress		cream
9. He	put		mixture		pot
it	looked	poisonous			stove
10. They	will be	tired			
they	arrive				
they	'll (will) want		rest		

NOTE:
In answers #4 and #5 in Exercise 29, and in answers #2, #3, #4, and #10 in Exercise 30 on page 127, "not" (and its contraction "n't") is an adverb (its "part of speech"), which functions here as part of the verb phrase and as part of the predicate (its "function of speech").

The ABCs of English Grammar

Exercise 30—Functions of Speech

	Subject	Predicate	Subject Complement	Direct Object	Indirect Object	Object of Prep.
1.	boy	rode		horse		meadow
	animal	could				
		enjoy		itself		
2.	He	did				
		know		ones		
	he	wanted				
3.	It	shall be done				
	minister	declared				
	I	can				
		guarantee				
	it	will				
		happen				
4.	group	had				
		expected		it		truck
	they	accepted		ride		Harbinder
5.	Mr. Smith	will				
		come				morning
						afternoon
	you	want		him		
	Mr. Brown	told		her		
6.	I	have				
		become	sick			food
	Rusty	stated				
	I	want		change		
	you	do				
		hear		me		
7.	they	had				
		medicated	people			Tuesday
	(they)	had		wish		visit

Subject	Predicate	Subject Complement	Direct Object	Indirect Object	Object of Prep.
8. family	burned		clothing		fire
it	was	filthy			use
9. all	looked				dog
efforts	were	useless			
10. Gail	has lent		money	Gary	
I	do think				
he	will pay		her		

Exercise 31—Parts of Speech

Noun =_____ Verb=_____ Adjective= ( ) Adverb= [ ]

Pronoun= ◯ Preposition= **P** Conjunction= **C**

Article= **A** Interjection= **I**

1. "Yeh!" the (young) man yelled when he felt the
power of the waves beneath him.

2. He did[n't] come, but I was[n't] (surprised).

3. The (golden) ruler belonged [only] to the king.

4. The family will give her everything before the year is finished.

5. [Speedily], [accurately], the (determined) mouse
[eagerly] grabbed the (mouldy) cheese.

6. He sang because he wanted the money so he could go on vacation.

7. (They) must have gone **P** into town, **P** for (none) of (us) has **P** seen (them.)

8. The (angry) **A** grandmother yelled, "Get [out] of (my) pantry, **P** (you) (little) brat!"

9. Susan went **P** beyond the ordinary **A** because (she) wanted **C** success for **P** Ron.

10. "Does[n't] (he) need **A** the money?" asked the **A** (disbelieving) father.

Exercise 32—Sentence Structure

1. "Michelle" is a popular name. (simple)

2. Jake and Bud ran and played in the park. (simple)

3. He went because his mother said she'd smack his face if he did[n't]. (complex. If you thought it was a compound-complex sentence, see the comment at the bottom of page 35 and the second set of examples on page 36.)

4. Since he had pleaded, she joined him, but she brought her friend, too. (compound-complex)

5. Although I like swordfish, there are other fish I prefer. (complex)

6. Whenever he giggled, he reminded me of a hyena, but I never told him. (compound-complex)

7. The Deans travelled by car, but the Smiths travelled by bus. (compound)

8. See Pat, if you can, but don't tell her I gave you her address. (There are two "you understood" subjects, and the sentence has two independent clauses and two dependent clauses. The relative pronoun "that" is understood before "I gave you her address," resulting in a compound-complex sentence.)

9. The young <u>woman</u> <u>has</u> little chance of making the most of herself, for <u>she</u> never <u>went</u> to school. (compound)

10. <u>I</u> can't <u>come</u> unless <u>I</u> <u>get</u> permission. (complex)

Exercise 33—Punctuation

1. I sang, I danced, I acted; I was the star of the evening. (Alternative corrections could be: 1) replace the semicolon with a suitable subordinating conjunction; 2) replace the semicolon and insert a comma followed by a suitable coordinating conjunction; 3) replace the semicolon with a period.)

2. He showed us the following materials: orlon; rayon; nylon; cotton; silk. (or...materials: orlon, rayon, nylon, cotton and silk.)

3. It was a tiresome parade of fashions, and I was sorry I attended the showing.

4. "Get out of here!" the naked man screamed. "Do you think you can just barge into my house without knocking?"

5. Chuck Johnson, the ambulance attendant, picked up the victim of an overdose at 5:20 a.m. Sunday.

6. The old man, who used to love chess, turned eighty-seven last week, and he celebrated with a toast to himself.

7. Mr. McKay said his address was 3456 Welling St., Auckland, New Zealand.

8. James looked at the crowd and smiled. "You'll never know what a great time I had here tonight," he said.

9. "I've got to go, but I don't have any idea of how to get to the bathroom," sobbed the little girl.

10. She bought a leather jacket, boys' shoes and men's pants.

11. "Mel Brooks was the person who said, 'Humor is just another defence against the universe,'" Martha Patterson said.

12. "It's true the robin is in its nest," she said, "but I don't have the courage to remove the body."

13. One of the most famous television shows was <u>All</u> <u>in</u> <u>the</u> <u>Family</u>.

14. He read the poem "The Rape of the Lock" and didn't understand a word.

15. <u>The</u> <u>London</u> <u>Times</u> is a famous newspaper, but I prefer others.

Exercise 34—The First Five Errors

1. Molly and she are going to have a good evening. (Faulty Subject-Verb Agreement)

2. He had a great time; I hope she did. (or) He had a great time, and I hope she did. (Comma Fault)

3. They like kissing and hugging. (or) They like to kiss and hug. (Faulty Parallelism)

4. With laughing eyes, she smacked his silly face. (Incomplete Sentence—any suitable subject and predicate could correct the error)

5. I lost the razor when I was in the store. (Ellipsis)

6. Kwame, plus all his family and friends, is going skiing this week-end. (Faulty Subject-Verb Agreement)

7. Jasper was a good tarantula, a safe tarantula, a healthy tarantula. (Faulty Parallelism)

8. Her marks are improving; she must be learning something. (or) Her marks are improving, so she must be learning something. (Comma Fault)

9. Down by the birth control clinic, I met the love of my life. (or) I met the love of my life down by the birth control clinic. (Incomplete Sentence—many other independent clauses could work just as well)

10. After hiking in California, I went riding in Oregon. (Incomplete Sentence)

Exercise 35—The First Five Errors

1. He should have been seen going running from the freaks. (Incomplete Sentence)

2. Both boys like to cruise and to party. (or) Both
   boys like cruising and partying. (Faulty Parallelism)

3. He goes to rock concerts, but I don't. (or) He goes to rock concerts;
   I don't. (Comma Fault)

4. My list of reasons is long. (Faulty Subject-Verb Agreement)

5. John eats organ meat, but I can't stand watching him. (Comma
   Fault. Alternative corrections might be, "John eats organ meat; I
   can't stand watching him." or "When John eats organ meat, I can't
   stand watching him.")

6. Queenie is bigger than any other dog in the kennel. (Ellipsis)

7. I had a love affair in the midst of a tropical heat wave.
   (Incomplete Sentence)

8. She loves to rap and to wrestle. (or) She loves rapping and
   wrestling. (Faulty Parallelism)

9. Each must return his or her book, or there will be a fine. (Comma
   Fault)

10. Neither the man nor his girlfriend is happy. (Faulty Subject-Verb
    Agreement)

Exercise 36—The Second Five Errors

1. After I called the airport, the flight was postponed. (Dangling
   Modifier. All that's needed is an appropriate subject.)

2. I came after she called me. (Tense Shift)

3. The children brought joy for you and me.
   (This is a Grammatical Error That Destroys Meaning because
   "for" is a preposition which must take an object which, in this
   sentence, is "me.")

4. He said, "Anyway, that's my story." (Illiteracy as there is no such word as "anyways.")

5. Her sister told Mary, "You will soon have your money." (Faulty Reference of Pronoun. We don't know in the original sentence who told whom.)

6. To enjoy jogging, one must wear shoes of good quality. (Dangling Modifier. Any suitable subject would make the sentence satisfactory.)

7. The teacher advised the student that the student would get AIDS unless he was more careful. (or, out of several possibilities) "You will get AIDS unless you are more careful," the teacher advised the student. (Faulty Reference of Pronoun)

8. "We will never betray our country," the man said. (Illiteracy. There are two negative words in the one clause. Only one is allowed.)

9. They smiled when he belched. (or) They smile when he belches. (Tense Shift. Both verbs must be in the same tense.)

10. He gave the present to them. (Grammatical Error That Destroys Meaning. The preposition "to" must take an object; "they" is a subject pronoun.)

Exercise 37—The Second Five Errors

1. The hunter went into the woods and saw a deer. (or) The hunter goes into the woods and sees a deer. (Tense Shift)

2. On entering the room, she saw a beautiful picture. (Dangling Modifier)

3. John and he are going. (Grammatical Error That Destroys Meaning)

4. He said he didn't get any. (Illiteracy)

5. She wore a ribbon in her red hair. (Faulty Reference of Pronoun. In the original sentence, the reader doesn't know whether "which" refers to her ribbon or her hair.)

6. When the pancakes are covered in syrup, you will enjoy the tasty dish. (Dangling Modifier)

7. Nate told his friend, "You should put some money into the machine." (Faulty Reference of Pronoun)

8. Carving carefully, he thought the turkey looked delicious. (Dangling Modifier)

9. The girl was terrified and began to resist. (Tense Shift)

10. My father scolded Harry and me. (Grammatical Error That Destroys Meaning)

Glossary

Antecedent	An antecedent is the word or group of words that a pronoun refers to.

Examples:

a. Percy said he could run a mile. ("Percy" is the antecedent of the pronoun "he.")

b. The firemen who saved the child are heroes. ("firemen" is the antecedent of the pronoun "who.")

Brackets	Except for certain technical uses, brackets are used for the insertion of a correction, comment, or added information.

Examples:

a. Original: He left Montral in 1996.

b. Correction: He left Montral [*sic*] in 1996.

(The *sic*, underlined, or written in italics, indicates that the writer is aware of the error in the original spelling of Montréal.)

b. He [Calvin Coolidge] had the reputation of being a man of few words.

c. Lady McBeth [and before she got into the hand thing] was never in the best of mental health.

Functions	The term "functions" as used in this book refers to subjects, predicates, subject complements, and the various objects (direct, indirect, object of the preposition).

Elliptical	Elliptical as used in this text refers to clauses or sentences in which easily supplied words are omitted, but understood.

Examples:

a. "Go away!" (here the omission is the subject "You," which is understood.)

b. He is the one I know. (the dependent clause, *that I know*, has the relative pronoun, *that*, omitted.)

Gender	The word "gender" refers to the classification of words as masculine, feminine, and neuter. In English, feminine pronouns (*she, her, hers*) are used for persons or things that are female (*Jane,*

bride, mare); masculine pronouns (*he, him, his*) are used for persons or things that are male (John, groom, stallion); neuter pronouns (*it, its*) are used for inanimate objects (and animals where the sex is not indicated).

Impersonal Usage

"Impersonal usage" specifies a verb occurring only in the third person singular with "it" as the indefinite subject.

Example:

It is a sunny day.

Italics

Italics refers to sloping print like this. Italic print may be used to indicate emphasis, to replace underlining, or to replace quotation marks (See page 63)

Origins

Coming into existence; beginning

Phonetic Pronunciation

"Phonetic" refers to speech sounds and their production. In the dictionary, for example, the entry word, "phonetic," would usually be followed by the phonetic spelling in parentheses. Note that the phonetic spelling, broken into syllables, is given as closely as possible to how the word sounds. The primary accent mark, ´, indicates the syllable that should get the greatest stress, or volume.

phonetic (feh net´ ik)

"Pronunciation" refers to the act or manner of saying words with reference to the production of sounds in a particular language.

Prefix

A prefix is a syllable, or syllables, joined to the beginning of a word to alter its meaning or to create a new word. Examples would be: **un**happy, **pre**history, **over**take.

Root Forms

The "root form" of a word is the base to which prefixes and suffixes are added. Examples would be dis**appear**ing, re**elect**ed.

Segment

A segment is a part which may be separated from the whole.

Suffix

A suffix is a syllable or a group of syllables joined to the end of a word to change its meaning, its function, or to form a new word. Examples would be: box**es**, dark**ness**, carry**ing**.

Index

The ABCs of English Grammar